Metal Gear Solid

Metal Gear Solid

Ashly &
Anthony Burch

Boss Fight Books
Los Angeles, CA
bossfightbooks.com

ISBN 13: 978-1-940535-09-8 (paperback)
First Printing: 2015
Second Printing: 2016
Third Printing: 2019

Series Editor: Gabe Durham
Book Design by Ken Baumann
Page Design by Adam Robinson

For Davey

CONTENTS

INTRODUCTION?

ANTHONY

Hideo Kojima loved movies.

"When I was a baby boy," he said in an interview with G4, "I was forced by my parents to watch movies, even before I knew who I was. I grew up on movies."

In college, Kojima got his hands on a Nintendo Famicom, the system that would eventually make its way to American shores as the Nintendo Entertainment System, and played *Super Mario Bros.* for the first time. Almost instantly, Kojima fell in love with video games and the possibilities they presented. If he could combine the fun of *Super Mario Bros.* with his vast knowledge of film, Kojima thought, he could make something fantastic.

In 1986, he joined Konami. Which was great, except he had no idea how to make video games. His job title was "planner," and he was the first person at Konami to hold it. His co-workers felt he was a fraud—some huckster who had talked his way into a sweet game development gig without possessing any actual knowledge of the process. Kojima's bosses also canceled his first project, "Lost World," which gave his co-workers more ammo. "Instead of saying 'Hi,'" Kojima told G4, "[people] would say, 'At least create ONE game before you die!'"

Evidently, Konami was full of dicks.

Shortly thereafter, Kojima came up with an idea for a military video game that, unlike all the other military games of its time, wasn't about fighting people. He wanted to make a game reminiscent of the film *The Great Escape*, one in which you spent more of your time running and hiding than facing the enemy head on.

His game, *Metal Gear*, was one of the first stealth video games ever made. *Metal Gear* introduces Solid Snake, a badass soldier who works for Big Boss, an even *more* badass soldier. While on a mission to rescue a bunch of POWs from a rogue fictional nation known as Outer Heaven, Snake finds out that Big Boss is actually a bad dude and has been leading Outer Heaven all along. Snake kills Big Boss (or so he thinks) and escapes. The game emphasized caution and observation over blind force.

And it was a hit. Released in Japan in 1987 for a computer called the MSX2, *Metal Gear* spawned a Nintendo port for the American market (which even got its own, noncanonical sequel, *Snake's Revenge*) and a Japan-only MSX2 sequel titled *Metal Gear 2: Solid Snake*.

Metal Gear 2: Solid Snake repeats the plot of the first game, this time set in the real-life location of Zanzibar. At the end, Big Boss shows back up because it turns out he'd never really died! And also Big Boss reveals he was Snake's father, and then Snake kills him again-but-for-real-this-time. If you actually *play Metal Gear 2*, some of that stuff doesn't happen, and is instead retconned bullshit from *Metal Gear Solid*. But don't—like, don't get distracted by that. It's fine. Just roll with it.

Fast-forward to 1994 and the release of the PlayStation. Kojima wanted to use the advanced 3D graphics offered by the PlayStation to bring Metal Gear into a new era. An era of cinematic storytelling and intense immersion. An era of high action and tactical espionage. An era of staring at butts.

In *Metal Gear Solid*, Solid Snake is once again brought out of retirement to combat a new threat to America and/or the world. A group of terrorists, comprised of psychopaths led by someone calling himself Liquid Snake, have taken control of a nuclear disposal facility and are threatening to launch some of the missiles at random targets unless they're given the remains of Big Boss. After arriving at the nuclear disposal facility on the Alaskan island of Shadow Moses, Snake sneaks around and shoots people for like ten or so hours, a good portion of which are super long cutscenes. Solid Snake and his team are confused—who the hell is this knockoff Snake, and why does he want the corpse of Big Boss?

Ash and I were born two years apart, me in 1988 and her in 1990. We got along about as well as any two siblings can get along. We both liked cartoons, we both liked video games,[1][2] and we both wanted to do something creative when we grew up even if we didn't know exactly what. We weren't completely the same— Ash liked anime, I liked John Carpenter movies. I tried my best to grow a healthy layer of badass stubble, Ash sang a lot of Celine Dion.

Later in life, my friends would tell me how envious they were of Ash's and my relationship. There were fights—you'll never *not* have fights as kids—but there were many more moments of real bonding. Hanging out, watching Toonami. Trying, and failing, to beat *Kirby Super Star* with 100% completion. We loved each other in that boring way that all siblings kinda-sorta *have* to love one another, but we were also pretty damned good friends.

•

I remember our first experience with *Metal Gear Solid*. Kind of.

---

1   **Anthony:** Even if I was generally better at them.

2   **Ash:** I WILL EAT YOUR SOUL COME AT ME.

We had a PlayStation demo disc with *Metal Gear Solid* on it. I don't remember exactly how or when we got it, but I remember it was one of the first discs we ever shoved into the squat, gray, plastic box that Ash received for her birthday. It was called the *Interactive Sampler* Volume 9, and it remains the greatest demo disc in existence. In addition to *Metal Gear Solid*, the disc included single levels from what would be some of the PlayStation's greatest titles: *Wild 9*, *Crash Bandicoot: Warped*, *MediEvil*, *Spyro the Dragon*, and *Brave Fencer Musashi*.[3] [4]

The *Interactive Sampler* demo of *MGS1* was the largest demo I've ever played. Starting at the beginning of the game and ending at the precise moment of the DARPA Chief's death, no chunk of gameplay had ever excited Ash and me in quite the same way. You had time to get immersed in the world and understand Snake's mission. You learned how to play at a reasonable, heavily-tutorialized pace rather than having to check the pause menu every six seconds to find out which button did what (as was the case with every other demo on the

---

3   **Anthony:** The sampler also had a demo for *NFL Gameday '99*. Every time you completed a game, the loading screen would show you a picture of the winning team's cheerleader. The Green Bay Packers had the cutest ones, so I intentionally lost over and over to see more of their cheerleaders. This is what I did before the Internet.

4   **Ash:** You forgot *Bust a Move 4* you FUCK.

sampler). Since the beginning is actually one of the most nonlinear sections of the game, the demo also implied the game's potential for exploration and freedom. Ash and I played through the demo a good half-dozen times before we realized that, holy *shit*, there was a *gun* hidden under a cargo truck! A gun! That they didn't shove in your face! We spent the next twenty minutes gleefully blasting away guards, marveling at the fact that a game would have the courage to hide something so important in a place where most players probably wouldn't find it.

Later, we found the alternate entrance into the base on the heliport's second floor. It didn't have that fun bit with the scared rats, sure, but it also didn't guarantee an alert when you inevitably walked in front of the surveillance camera that protected the other entrance. "Oh man," we shouted, "the guards toss a grenade into the vent if they see you hiding in there whaaaaat."

We experimented with different ways of completing the demo. Could you get through without alerting anybody? Get through without leaving a single guard alive? Could you lead a guard on a wild goose chase just by tricking him into following your footsteps in the snow?

Not to mention all the intriguing questions posed by the demo's cliffhanger. The DARPA Chief dies of a seemingly random heart attack. A redheaded woman bangs on the wall in the next cell. Years before *Lost*, the climax of *Metal Gear Solid's* demo had us rapt—this was our first dose of mystery-centric storytelling. Why did that guy suddenly die? Did Snake kill him? Who was that redhead, and why did she mutter "that card key…" when she heard the DARPA chief mention it?

We rented the full game as soon as our parents allowed us to, and blitzed through most of it sitting on the end of Ash's bed.[5]

I mention this not only to indulge in nostalgia, but to give context for what you're about to read. Ash and I are, to put it bluntly, going to shit on *Metal Gear Solid.* We'll talk about flaws in its story. We'll talk about how it's sexist and regressive. We'll talk about how, despite its reputation, it's actually a pretty bad stealth game. Today, *MGS1* represents many things we either disagree with, find irritating, or actively fight against in our jobs as critics and creators.

But: *Metal Gear Solid* was the perfect game to Ash and me as kids. We love it with the part of our hearts protected by Kevlar nostalgia. In the chapters to come, we're going to try to remember that love and we hope you'll do the same.

---

5   **Ash:** Our parents assume that every game is some variation on *Super Mario,* otherwise they probably wouldn't have let us play *MGS1* that young. Trying to explain *Borderlands* to them is difficult.

SNAKE?

The snow crunches under my feet as I approach the guard from behind. He makes a "hurk" noise as I grapple him, then makes it six more times as I tighten my grip. With a sharp crack and a relieved-sounding sigh, he crumples to the ground.

"Ah," I think. "The old hurk-hurk-hurk-hurk-hurk-hurk-hurk-snap-ahhh maneuver. Gets them every time."

This is my job. They call me Snake. I have many skills: solo infiltration, tactical stealth... the works. It's been less than twelve hours since my old friend Colonel Campbell pulled me out of retirement, and I'm here on Shadow Moses Island to complete a vital mission. A terrorist named Liquid Snake has taken over the nuclear disposal facility on this island, and is threatening to launch a nuke at Washington. I'm to get in, save a few key hostages, and stop the launch.

They called me because nobody else is up for the job. They called me because I'm the most experienced, most deadly, and most reliable operative in the history of the Special Forces. They called me because I am the greatest soldier who ever lived—a legend in the flesh.

Moving past the corpse, I see a surveillance camera. I can tell it is a surveillance camera because it is a surveillance camera.

"A surveillance camera?" I say incredulously.

I am Solid Snake. I am the stupidest man in the world.

ANTHONY

Why is it that, unlike so many other stealth game protagonists, Solid Snake is easily the most beloved? He's been listed as one of the greatest video game characters of all time by *Electronic Gaming Monthly*, Empire Online, GameSpot, and others. Millions of people love the Thief and Splinter Cell games, but I've rarely seen anyone cosplay as Sam Fisher. I seldom see Garrett on lists of the most memorable game heroes. What is it about Snake— an unapologetic rip-off of Kurt Russell's Snake Plissken character from *Escape From New York*—that has captured the gaming community's imagination for *25 years*?

On the face of things, Snake's appeal is obvious. He's a Cool, Gruff Loner who Takes No Prisoners while Doing What Needs To Be Done. He shaves just enough to maintain some haggard stubble, and has a voice you could only get by smoking cigarettes since you were in the womb. But these aspects of Snake don't add up to a character, they add up to an action movie trope, and a pretty generic one at that.

At the same time, Snake is almost the opposite of the Snake Plisskens of the world. He doesn't have any cool one-liners, for instance. His most memorable line from *MGS1* is, "I think at any time, any place, people can fall in love with each other," and people sure as hell don't remember that line because it's *cool*. He's also not very smart or capable: Every single Metal Gear game starring Snake involves him getting screwed over, used, tricked, and bamboozled, all while being *completely surprised* that said bamboozling has happened, again.

Yet even while Kojima tries to convince Metal Gear fans that, no, the whole series is actually about Big Boss, many of us still cling tight to our love for the guy who repeats things he's just been told as questions *78 separate times* throughout the course of the first *Metal Gear Solid*.[6]

So, what is it that makes Solid Snake so memorable?

ASH

To call Snake complex would imply a certain level of intention on Kojima's part that I'm not sure exists, but it would be inaccurate to call him simple. He's simultaneously detached and empathetic. He's both highly capable and tortuously oblivious.

A likely explanation for these inconsistencies is that Snake is a stand-in for the player, so he needs to help

---

6   **Snake:** "Super baby method?"

progress narrative and aid characterization whenever possible. This results in some pretty weird juxtapositions, like Snake telling Meryl, a fellow soldier and his love interest in the game, that he doesn't care about anyone, then asking Mei Ling, the mission's soliton radar expert, in-depth questions about her family over a codec[7] conversation five seconds later.[8]

Which makes it doubly embarrassing to admit why Snake resonated with me as a prepubescent girl, and why I'm oddly loyal to him to this day: He was my first real crush.[9] I understood that admitting that I liked a video game character would get me filleted by my peers, so while my friends fawned over their preferred member of *NSYNC, I held a silent torch for Snake and told everyone I had the hots for JC.[10]

What's a bit harder to pinpoint is why this particular gruff, take-no-nonsense-except-for-all-the-times-he-takes-nonsense protagonist caught my eye in the first place. To young-Ash, Snake's appeal was wrapped up

---

7 **Ash:** *Metal Gear Solid*'s fancy word for radio.

8 **Anthony:** I wonder if this is because Snake immediately wants to fuck Mei Ling, whereas Meryl is somebody he has to warm up to. If you actually accept that logic, it means that Snake's questions about Mei Ling's family are really disingenuous—he's feigning interest so Mei Ling will remain interested in him.

9 **Ash:** The plot thickens for those three guys on YouTube who think I'm a lesbian.

10 **Ash:** I was on the wrong side of history.

in his seeming complexity. Snake was stoic. Mysterious. Well-loved by the ladies. A protector. A hero. That emotionally distant, secretly devoted type. At a young age, I was conditioned to idealize that sort of man—the man you have to prove yourself to, the man hiding behind a wall of apathy you have to crack. Certainly the narrative of the game suggests as much. His libido is so strong that Meryl falls in love with him having spent five minutes in his presence. Keep in mind that this is *after* Snake asks, voice dripping with condescension, "Are you sure you can do this, rookie?" and, "Do you know how to fire that thing, little girl?" Take notes, gentlemen.

I've grown out of my predilection for the Snake paradigm of men, but the idea that emotionally distant, brooding, misogynist protectors are ideal mates hasn't exactly been excised from our culture. More recently, *Twilight* has offered us the model abusive turd that is Edward Cullen. His presence is an actual, physical, constant threat to Bella, and he's the goddamn Han Solo of my generation. Han was rough and tumble, but he sure as shit never broke into Leia's bunk so he could watch her sleep.

There are examples of this type of man in all media, and they're almost always cast as the protagonist. Snake was my particular brand of emotionally inept, condescending hunk, but ladies the world over have their pick.

ANTHONY

I certainly didn't have a crush on Snake when I first played *MGS1* (I didn't find out I was bisexual until adulthood),[11] but I definitely wanted to *be* him. He, along with a handful of other fictional characters (Ash from *Evil Dead*, Batman, Dwight from *Sin City*) exemplified masculinity. Snake in particular represented two concepts that were both appealing to me:

1. He was a stoic badass, just like I wanted to be.
2. He was a hopeless romantic, just like I actually was.

When you're a young boy, your culture trains you to have the fewest number of emotions possible beyond "angry," "determined," or "hungry." You want to attract women, but also be enough of a loner-type that you don't need one. And, through all of it, you desperately want people to think you're cool without them knowing just *how* desperately you want them to think you're cool.

Above all else, Snake is *in control*. If he wants a girl to sleep with him, she'll wanna sleep with him. If he wants to treat a girl as nothing more than an enemy, then that's all she'll be. As someone who spent the majority of his childhood falling in love with people he absolutely did

---

11 **Anthony:** "She admitted to having a crush on a fictional character," he thought. "She's winning the admitting-private-things-in-public game. *I've gotta one-up that fucker.*"

not want to fall in love with, I was especially drawn to this aspect of Snake's character.

And yet he's got a softer side. Shortly after it is revealed that Meryl is effectively in love with Snake, we also learn that Snake cares deeply about her too. This is ludicrous, of course. At the time that this revelation occurs, they've known each other for about an hour.

Up to this point, Snake has taken every possible opportunity to point out that he's not interested in romantic entanglements. What kind of an immature, emotionally stunted, inconsistent weirdo would behave like this? In moments like this, Snake acts like a... like a...

Well, exactly like a ten-year-old boy. The same sort of ten-year-old boy who might pick up a game with a hardcore-sounding name like *Metal Gear Solid*.[12]

Take the "people can fall in love with each other at any time" line I mentioned earlier.

After a high-octane helicopter escape sequence, Otacon (Snake's good-natured scientist buddy who assists him throughout the series) tracks him down for a little heart-to-heart.

"There's something I've really gotta ask you," Otacon says. "It's why I followed you up this far." He adjusts

---

12   **Ash:** Which, appropriately, also sounds like a name that a ten-year-old would've come up with, because those three words make no sense together.

his glasses, exuding as much nervousness as a 32-bit polygonal character possibly can.

"Do you think love can bloom, even on a battlefield?"

Without hesitation or irony, Snake responds: "Yeah, I do. I think at any time, any place… people can fall in love with each other."

Is this inconsistent with Snake's character as it has been presented thus far? Yes. Is the dialogue clunkier than a bagful of wrenches? Yes. But as silly as that conversation is, it reveals the duality that makes Snake so memorable: He's a super-cool badass and a lovelorn dork at the exact same time.

Snake possesses all of the external unidimensionality that I aspired to, while secretly harboring the naive romanticism that determined most of my behavior from ages eight to twenty. He was someone I could simultaneously relate to and worship—someone who reflected who I was, and who I someday wanted to be.

ASH

What's interesting about Snake as a role model is that, in actuality, he's sexually illiterate. Much like the ten-year-olds who worship him, Snake is confused by sex and even afraid of it. The macho-man Casanova exterior is a facade that hides feelings of uncertainty.

Revisiting *MGS1* as an adult, there's a clear element of over-performance, posturing, and/or fearfulness in

Snake's interactions with, well, *every* woman in the game. Snake hits on Mei Ling and Naomi within moments of each other. They're also standing right next to each other and can *hear all of his conversations*. Snake just landed in the middle of a snowstorm, there are armed men surrounding him, he's trying to stop terrorists from setting off a bomb, and *now* is the time to tell Mei Ling that she's got a cute voice? These opening codec conversations feel like they were written by a thirteen-year-old bursting with puberty hormones: bad pick-up lines work on two hot girls, and they don't care that you're hitting on both of them at the same time? Sweet! It's like *MGS1* is its own best fanfic.

But Snake doesn't hit on *every* woman he meets. In fact, the two women in the game who are *dripping with sexuality*—Nastasha, the mission's weapons expert, and Sniper Wolf, a sniper in the terrorist group—he has no interest in. Sniper Wolf I get: The first time Snake meets her, she shoots Meryl a bunch of times and almost kills her. One could see how that would be a buzzkill. But he has the same relationship with Nastasha as he does with Mei Ling: She's an aid in a remote location, an attractive woman, and her voice perpetually sounds as if she is mid- or immediately post-coitus. But Snake is cordial with her. No come-ons, no odd comments. Just business. She's the one person who seems as if she'd be open to a little grab-ass between missions, and he doesn't say anything even remotely suggestive. Is he intimidated by Nastasha? Afraid? It's much easier to be playful with Mei Ling—who seems as bashful about flirtation as a young girl might be—than a grown-ass woman who is down to bump uglies because that's what adults *do*. The immediacy of the sexuality, the possibility that that a woman would actually be *willing*, seems too much for him.

Things get even more complicated when we reach the boss fight with Psycho Mantis, a psychic with telekinetic powers. To combat Snake, Mantis performs such mystical feats as making your controller vibrate with his mind and reading the data stored on your memory card.[13]

But in the litany of tricks at his disposal, the first thing Psycho Mantis does is possess Meryl and make her sexually proposition Snake. Right out of the gate. Possession → "Snake make love to me." Forcing a young woman to make sexual advances on someone against her will is *definitely* disturbing—I'm with you on that one, Mantis. But you tend to open with your strongest attack. One would think the most traumatic thing for Snake to see would be Meryl pointing a gun at her own head, but Mantis doesn't threaten that until much later. He opens with Meryl asking Snake for sex. And, being a psychic, he can *read Snake's mind*. So when he

---

13   **Ash:** That shit might seem dorky now, but when you're ten it fucks you *up*.

popped into the "man-this-stuff-is-spooky, I-hope-an-evil-psychic-never-sees-this" part of Snake's brain, Psycho Mantis found that "Meryl asking me for sex" was ranked above "Meryl killing herself."

Did you ever know that kid in elementary school who would talk a big game about seeing a girl's boobs, but who froze up at the sight of any actual, adult sexuality?

Swap kid-in-elementary-school for tactical-espionage-agent and you've got the general feeling of the Psycho Mantis boss fight.

This idea of Snake as a sexually stunted pseudo-child is actually consistent with Snake's backstory. Snake is the clone of a super soldier and, since he was a child, has only known life on the battlefield. Being bred to kill doesn't leave much room for healthy sexual development.

Metal Gear Solid was a game that was marketed toward boys, and Snake was a protagonist many boys (like Anthony) aspired to be like. Whether the inclusion of Snake's schizophrenic relationship with sexuality was an accident or not, it ends up falling right in line with the stage of sexual development of its core audience. In that sense, Snake could speak a lot more about the experience of a straight cis young boy—what he values,[14]

---

14   **Anthony:** Boobies.

what he dislikes,[15] what he aspires to[16]—than might be immediately obvious. While Snake's personality reads as inconsistent and his ruminations on life and love might seem absurd to an adult gamer, the game's young male demographic might find that fear and confusion about sexuality are more relatable than anything else Psycho Mantis could throw Snake's way.

Which invites the question: What is Snake teaching young dudes about how they construct their values? Characters like Snake (and Batman and Max Payne and Master Chief and on and on) are essentially teaching young boys that being emotional and vulnerable isn't cool. It's discouraging to me that Anthony's most visible and impacting role models growing up were all emotionless misogynists. Which isn't to say that video games and other forms of media *create* misogynists, but these sorts of narratives perpetuate destructive ideas of what a man should be. They promote excising vulnerability and emotionality from one's relational repertoire. They equate "feeling" with "weakness." This false comparison only makes it harder for boys to form meaningful relationships, be competent leaders, compassionate fathers, and to know when and how to admit fault.

---

15   **Anthony:** Not-boobies.

16   **Anthony:** World Champion Boobie Toucher Hall of Fame.

More optimistically, though, Snake teaches us that boys don't necessarily look up to guys who are *just* macho beefcakes. Snake can talk about love, reflect wistfully on life and loss, and (eventually) learn to appreciate Meryl earnestly and openly. Boys are complex human beings with nuanced desires and interests. Snake, although flawed in many ways, is far from simple. So what if we pushed him to be even more complex? What if we ditched the tough-guy lone wolf act and went all in on tactically-capable-but-emotionally-sensitive Snake? What if we leaned on those vulnerable aspects of his personality that invite relatability, without also doubling down on machismo? Who's to say boys wouldn't respond to it?

Hell, who's to say they wouldn't *prefer* it?

•

ANTHONY

There are two Hideo Kojimas.

One Kojima injects every Metal Gear Solid game with earnest if overbearing discussions of nuclear disarmament, the morality of genetic experimentation, the nature of warfare, and the difference between patriotism and terrorism.

The other Kojima lets you call Rose in *Metal Gear Solid 4* and shake your SIXAXIS controller to make her boobs jiggle.

One Kojima is interested in genetic and memetic legacies, and predicted the rise of social media and information overload years before Twitter.

The other Kojima helped design a sniper whose breasts are so large and exposed that she caused controversy before the game in which she appears even had a release date.

One explores the nature of control and identity through the player's natural inclination to role-play.

The other thought it'd be funny to include a super-intelligent monkey who is addicted to soda.

Yin/Yang. Solid/Liquid. Postmodernism/monkey burps.

Then again, this duality can be found in an even more obvious place: the player's mind. In any game, the player is an agent of chaos. In one moment, they might agonize over whether to succumb to torture and let a supporting character die. In another, they might run around in circles for an hour. In another, they might stare at a blocky polygon butt. The player is a million different things throughout the course of any video game.

Snake, like so many other video game protagonists, is in a weird spot. As the game is so eager to remind us, he's a fantastic soldier: an experienced, tactically brilliant warrior feared by his enemies and idolized by his allies.

The player, on the other hand, is easily confused, easily bored, and happy to walk Snake over a trap door just to see what happens. We *MGS1* fans love to mock Snake's propensity to repeat things told to him in the form of a question, but he only ever did it for the player's benefit. Every bewildered utterance of "Nanomachines?" or "Secret black project?" served almost exclusively to help the player's journey through a complex plot that would only get more convoluted with time.

Yet, Snake isn't *just* a stand-in for the player, and *Metal Gear Solid* isn't *just* a typical wish fulfillment delivery device. Sure, every single character in the game comments on Snake's prowess as a soldier (even the ones who want to kill you), but as the story chugs along, it works harder and harder to separate You the Player from Snake the Character.

Snake begins to diverge from the player shortly after he is tortured via electrocution by Revolver Ocelot, another member of the FOXHOUND terrorist group who—surprise, surprise—is great with a revolver. After the first round of torture, Snake reveals a shocking piece of information: Big Boss, his former mentor and the man he killed in the previous Metal Gear game, was actually his father! Snake and the game both attempt to pass this revelation off as something other than the obvious retcon it is. (Big Boss says nothing about any familial connection to Snake when they face each other down at the end of *Metal Gear 2: Solid Snake*, and Kojima has since admitted that he cooked up the cloned son subplot to raise the narrative stakes in *Metal Gear Solid*.) But for the first time in the game, Snake reveals that he knew something we didn't.

Several times, the game approaches agency with an inconsistency that borders on random. Near *Metal Gear Solid*'s halfway point, Snake decides to shoot a wounded Sniper Wolf in the face without giving the player even the illusion of choice (as *MGS3*'s ending does, where players are at least forced to hit a single button to kill the main baddie and move the story forward). A few hours earlier, though, the player was allowed to decide whether Snake would let Meryl die.

This is pretty damned inconsistent. Sure, Snake's a tough guy who shows mercy only through headshots, but *you* get to decide whether he's suddenly got the pain tolerance of an infant. He'll still save the day whether Meryl is dead or not but you can decide for yourself *just* how much he values Meryl. (Until the sequels, anyway—Kojima made Meryl's survival canon.)[17]

On one hand, most third-person action games are full of this kind of avatar dissonance. When I play *Uncharted* and brutally snap someone's neck, I can't help but feel uncomfortable when Nathan Drake loudly laughs and

---

17   **Ash:** "Fuck your choices!" *Kojima dons glasses, jet skis into sunset.*

cracks a joke at the noise it made. When I play *God of War*, I'm meant to find Kratos's brutality distancing and awful even as I further it through my actions. Game designers and writers are more than happy to use the third-person perspective so you can have your agency-cake and eat it too: The players are themselves sometimes and the pre-authored protagonist at other times.

But *Metal Gear Solid* is *extremely* interested in highlighting that disconnect instead of attempting to hide it, as other games do.[18] At the game's climax, Snake's old nemesis Gray Fox sacrifices himself so Snake will have a shot at destroying Metal Gear REX, an enormous nuclear weapon shaped like a mech that roars like a dinosaur.[19] Exposing himself to the Metal Gear's attacks, Fox lets himself get cornered so that REX will focus on him.

"Now," he shouts. "Fire the stinger!"

Fox knowingly puts himself in a position to get killed just so Snake can have this chance—it'd be idiotic not to take it, even if it means the stinger missile will also kill him.

But.

---

18   **Anthony:** For instance, pedestrians in *Grand Theft Auto IV* will never actually die. Shooting them multiple times or running them over will simply put them into a wounded state that looks very much like death until an ambulance drives up and revives them. Presumably, this system was implemented to reduce the dissonance between Niko Bellic's story of redemption and the player's potential love of slaughter.

19   **Ash:** Kojima!

"It's no good," Snake says as you slap the square button repeatedly. "I can't do it!"

No matter how many times you press the fire button throughout Gray Fox's (unskippable) minute-long valediction, Snake will respond in the same way: "It's no good—I can't do it."[20] Sorry, player: You may be willing to sacrifice Fox to save the day, but Snake isn't. Just in case you forgot, this isn't your story—you may have determined Snake's strength in the face of torture, but you don't get to decide how much he cares about Gray Fox.

Usually, agency overrides such as this arise when a video game wants to show the player something the player can't be trusted to do themselves. If the designer wants the hero to unleash hell in a way that the player can't accomplish with their in-game verbs, they show the hero doing it in a cutscene. If the writer wants the player character to do something morally ambiguous or horrific to progress the plot, but they're worried the player won't bring themselves to do it, the designer will override the player's agency and force them to act in accordance with the script.[21]

---

20   **Anthony:** Which, if you hammer the button as frequently as I did, results in a rapid-fire loop of those seven angrily delivered words.

21   **Anthony:** When done well, this kind of narrative design results in *BioShock*'s climactic face-off against Andrew Ryan. When done poorly, you get *Modern Warfare 2*'s "No Russian."

Snake's refusal to kill Gray Fox doesn't fit into either of these categories. You *want* to kill Gray Fox—hell, maybe *need* to, depending on how badly injured you are at this point in the boss fight—and Snake steadfastly refuses to do the one thing that would be the most intelligent, the most dramatically appropriate, and the most badass.

By refusing the player's wishes and *not* killing Gray Fox, Snake proves himself a far more nuanced, empathetic, and sensitive character than the game's initial chest-thumping hero worship would lead us to believe. The "love on a battlefield" monologue tried to convince us of this with mixed results, but Snake's ultimate refusal to kill Gray Fox proves it in the most fourth-wall-breaking of ways.

Unlike most game series whose protagonists get more brutal and "heroic" as time goes on,[22] Snake gets more nuanced through the years, increasingly challenging his grizzled hero status.

Throughout his section of *Metal Gear Solid 2*, Snake is at his most gruff and emotionless. But as the game begins to unveil its labyrinthine thematic structure, however, things get more interesting. At the end of *MGS2*, Raiden throws away the set of dog tags embossed

---

22 **Anthony:** By the time we reached *Splinter Cell: Blacklist*, Sam Fisher had turned from a sarcastic government stooge into a Jack Bauer-esque torturer.

with his player-given name.[23] This ending makes it clear that *MGS2* is actually about the dangers of hero worship. Both Raiden and the player are suckered into working for the bad guys out of a blind desire to be as cool and as tough as Solid Snake. Kojima's decision to trick players into thinking they'd be playing as Solid Snake throughout the entire game, only to bait-and-switch them into a game about an androgynous, irritating upstart was the ultimate expression of this idea.[24] *I get that you wanna be Snake*, Kojima implies, *but that's no way to live your life.*

Despite all his empathy in *MGS1*, Snake's gruff detachedness reaches almost sociopathic levels in *MGS2*. When Vamp, a terrorist obsessed with dramatically licking his knife, brutally murders Emma Emmerich, the little sister of Otacon, Snake shows almost no sympathy for her plight and tells Otacon to stop being a little *bitch* and save some hostages because that's what men do. Then, five minutes later, he seemingly betrays Raiden and knocks him comatose. Granted, this betrayal ended up being part of a larger plan to save Raiden and

---

23   **Anthony:** In my story, Raiden's dog tags read "Buttfart McMahon."

24   **Anthony:** It's become sexy to pretend that *MGS2* is a misunderstood masterpiece because of its thematic complexity, narrative weirdness, and refusal to give the player what they want. NOPE. Meta-commentary or not, game still sucks.

win the day, but *Jesus Christ, dude*—you couldn't have told me you were going to knock me unconscious and take all my stuff? I woke up *literally holding my dick in my hands.*

Metal Gear Solid 4 further deconstructs Snake as a hero. In fact, the entire game seems designed to make you pity the decrepit Old Snake. If you stay crouched for too long, he'll suffer back pains and audibly complain about them. When he meets Meryl, she tells him that he's a broken down piece of shit and she can't believe she ever saw anything in him. Nearly every single plot event serves to make him sad, confused, or hopeless. Only one moment in the game makes Snake happy: When talking to the buxom Naomi, Snake pretends to accidentally drop a cigarette on the ground so he can look up Naomi's skirt as he bends down to pick it up.[25]

If *MGS1* were the only Metal Gear Solid game in existence, it'd be even easier to look back at Snake as nothing more than another generic military hero. However, *Metal Gear Solid 2* and *4*'s deconstructions of Snake's hero legend show that there's more to him than meets the eye. *Metal Gear Solid 3* goes as far as jettisoning Solid Snake entirely and focusing on Snake's archenemy, Big Boss. *MGS3* tries hard to humanize Big Boss and ultimately make him more likable than

---

25   **Anthony:** Kojima!

even Solid Snake. By the time *Metal Gear Solid 4* rolls around, Snake's role as the hero of the franchise has been almost completely undermined.

ASH

Given this evolution of Snake's character over the course of the franchise, perhaps Kojima realized after the release of *MGS1* that it wasn't the best move to have a generation of impressionable young boys play a dude who 75% of the time amounts to a misogynist dick.

Or maybe he realized that a more nuanced protagonist is more interesting than just adding *another* gruff macho-man to the roster of video game heroes. Or maybe he created Snake to be an analogue to his presumed audience, and developed the character with them as they grew up, showing that he respects the intelligence of the fanbase.

But then of course he was like, "look bro u can make dat girl's boobs jiggle by shaking ur controller lolz."

So I guess it all evens out.

In the end.

TONE?

ASH

I remember the first time Anthony and I saw the elevator scene in *MGS1*. We were sitting at the edge of my bed, enthralled. I was exhausted from anxiety and a constant string of high-octane battles, and was looking forward to a bit of a respite before plunging into another firefight. To which *Metal Gear Solid* said: *Fuck you Ashly Burch get spooked.*

And spooked is exactly what I got.

The infamous elevator is located in a generic building on the base that sits narratively between the Hind D fight and the second Sniper Wolf boss battle. Initially, when the player tries to use the lift, it won't budge, and Snake has to ask Otacon to get it moving again. After a quick pop outside to get some fresh air and commit some close-but-no-cigar fratricide against Liquid Snake, the leader of the terrorist group and your main antagonist, the elevator is magically functional. Otacon admits that he doesn't know why it's working.

As a kid, I assumed that the inoperable elevator was just an indication that there was another plot beat we had to complete before we could use the lift. Games, particularly games in the 90s, before "open world" became the gold standard, would often lock off certain parts of a level or a map until you finished the current task. There was usually a narrative justification for it— you need a key to unlock this door, you need a specific power to open this gate, etc. As a wee-Ashly, I thought this was just a particularly inelegant implementation of the same idea. The elevator is broken → I must need to do something else → oh, a helicopter fight → explode helicopter → cool, elevator is working. Bingo bango, no big deal.

I was a sitting duck.

When you enter the elevator, a loud buzzing sound goes off. Snake is confused by it, but Snake is confused by everything, so Anthony and I just disregarded it.

Then, Otacon calls you on the codec. He tells you that there were five stealth suit prototypes—full-body outfits that make the wearer invisible—in his lab. He took one much earlier in the game to wear around the facility, leaving four unclaimed suits. He explains that he went back to the lab to grab one of the prototypes for

Snake, only to find that all four of them were missing. Not invisible—missing.

The elevator's whirring fades as the elevator comes to a halt. Everything is silent, save for Otacon's voice. He says that there is something strange about the elevator as well, like someone is "intentionally holding it."

Snake catches on. His voice has a distinct ripple of urgency as he asks if the weight limit warning went off when Otacon was riding the elevator. *Shit! That was the buzzing noise we heard? Oh god oh god oh god.* Otacon confirms that the weight limit is off, but that Snake's measly 140 lbs is well under the 650-lb limit for the elevator.

The angry furrow in Snake's brow deepens and the gravel in his voice sharpens as he growls, "It would take at least *five people* to go over that limit."

Suddenly, Otacon's face fills the codec screen as he shouts, "The guys who stole my stealth prototypes are in there with you!"

ANTHONY

I can't understate just how surprising this moment is. Presumably to save animation budget, most of the codec portraits almost never moved in any significant way. Apart from the constant mouth flaps and the odd chuckle, the characters are basically static. Until this moment, that is, when the codec camera is suddenly *inches* from Otacon's panic-stricken face.[26]

ASH

What follows is a pretty straightforward fight that doesn't much deviate from any of the gameplay previously established in the game. But Anthony and I were *terrified*. The sound design, as well as the simple choice to have Otacon's face engulf the codec screen, was so effectively frightening that the tension and stakes of the fight were immediately heightened. For all intents and purposes, the elevator is just a small setpiece for an action beat leading into yet another action beat. But even though the action is mechanically identical to all the other gunfights in the game, the simple, brief genre swap from action to horror made an otherwise mundane fight instantly engaging and terrifying.

•

ANTHONY

I still remember the blood-soaked hallway.

After getting past a hallway of poison gas and electrified floors, Snake is suddenly confronted with a

---

26 **Anthony:** What's unclear is just how Snake sees anyone on the codec's "camera." The game tells us that the codec is a little microchip thingy implanted in Snake's ear. Where are the portraits coming from?

scene of unprecedented carnage. Corpses line the path leading to Otacon's office. Impact patterns dot the walls. Blood stains the corridor and pools on the ground. Even before Snake turns the corner and sees an unfortunate genome soldier getting impaled by an invisible ninja, the hallway o' blood has set a tone. It puts the player on edge and clearly foreshadows something new, scary, and brutal. Unlike many modern games, Kojima wisely chose to save any explicit depictions of ultraviolence until they would be most useful. Because the player hasn't seen this much blood throughout the rest of the game combined,[27] the hallway does its job.[28]

Today, it's easy to take blood-soaked hallways for granted. The player turns a corner, sees a bunch of corpses, and the music gets all scary—we've done it a thousand times in a thousand different first-person shooters. After *BioShock*, dozens of game devs realized the power of environmental narrative, and since 99% of video games are about killing and being killed by things, "environmental narrative" now translates to into: "It appears a large number of men died in this particular area, making sure to fall in highly dramatic poses while

---

27   **Anthony:** The enemies Snake shoots emit a mere puff of red, and Revolver Ocelot's arm stump spurts about a tablespoon of blood before he clamps it down.

28   **Ash:** Thinking about the first time I saw it and how deathly quiet it was still gives me the willies.

splashing their blood onto the walls in visually arresting patterns. Also somebody probably wrote, 'They're going to kill us' on the wall with their own blood."

Metal Gear Solid, on the other hand, understood restraint.[29]

Kojima and his team managed to make a truly scary game without resorting to jump scares or ludicrous amounts of violence.

A lot of the scares come from the fact that Snake is, by nature, a disempowered character. Since *MGS1* is a stealth game rather than a balls-out action brawler, threats against Snake's life have more meaning. The elevator scene was and remains legitimately terrifying because *Snake is vulnerable*. In the levels leading up to this big moment, Snake has fled from dozens of baddies or mown about twenty down with Meryl at his side, but he's never been trapped alone in a small and inescapable space. The threat of having to fight four invisible dudes in an enclosed area actually holds weight because close quarters combat (at least, before Snake becomes a hand-to-hand master in later Metal Gear Solid games) is not Snake's strong suit.

Contrast this with something like Monolith's *FEAR*, where your character can jump-kick marines in the face while firing pistols from each hand. You're so friggin' powerful that the game's constant attempts at scares and

---

29   **Ash:** This is probably the only time anyone will ever say this about *Metal Gear Solid*.

spookery ring hollow. Why should I be scared of a little girl when I have a slow-motion ability? *FEAR*'s many jump scares and sophisticated lighting tricks are not even a tenth as frightening as *Metal Gear Solid*'s scariest moments.

Of all the locales in the Metal Gear Solid games, Shadow Moses is still one of the series's greatest. It's no coincidence that the penultimate act of *Metal Gear Solid 4* sees Snake return to the fateful nuclear disposal facility where the story began, and that the subsequent level is chock-full of downright ludicrous fanservice.

The game can be uptempo and fun when it wants to be but most every level sees you confronted with subtle, unnerving background music. The first level of the game, the loading dock, surprises the player with its music choice. The player presses the Start button to begin the game, hears a gunshot, and then watches the first cut scene fade in only to hear… a haunting, Gaelic opera song. Rather than a rip-roaring, adrenaline-pumping adventure score, the first sound the player hears is sad, almost funereal chanting. Once the player gains control, the ambient score consists of a quiet, ghostlike thrum occasionally punctuated by percussive stabs.[30] It's a spy game scored with haunting opera. It's

---

30   **Anthony:** It's also probably no coincidence one of the game's more elaborate secrets sees much of the development team hidden throughout the base as creepy-ass ghosts who can only be seen through the lens of Snake's digital camera.

a military action game that takes place in a haunted house.

ASH

And Shadow Moses is the only setting in the franchise that is so deliberately scary. The rest of the games in the series are interested in projecting realism and brutality—visceral, physical settings that give the sequels a grittier feel. But Shadow Moses is almost surreal in its spookiness. When you step into the ruins of Shadow Moses in *MGS4*, it's like revisiting a dream—or, more accurately, a nightmare. Part of that is achieved by the game's color scheme. The walls and floors are almost exclusively blue and gray. No distinct colors or contrasts stick out, save for the lava area at the end of the game. When I think of the settings in *MGS2*, my memories are a lot more colorful. Suddenly, the world—the cargo areas, the suspension bridges, the comm towers—had browns, whites, reds, and greens in it—who knew? This realistic color palette made it much easier to think of the settings in *MGS2, MGS3,* and *MGS4* as spaces that actually existed. Shadow Moses, on the other hand, with its almost monochromatic design, felt like it was constructed to be foreign and scary and cold and dangerous—a hermetically sealed spooky capsule. This could have been an economical choice on the part of the developers, but given the tonal trajectory of the series, the color palette and haunting design makes sense.

If you started playing *Metal Gear Solid* at age eight or ten like we did, and ended with *MGS4* at ages eighteen and twenty, then the franchise covered a pretty hefty chunk of your own maturation. As a result, *MGS4* tackled some heftier subject matters while still being mostly inane and working in a lot of diarrhea jokes. Like, a lot of them.[31]

The realistic world of *Metal Gear Solid 4*—which takes place, in part, in the Middle East where *actual* wars are being fought—made sense for that game. It felt like an older, wisened extension of the first game, and matched the growth that Anthony and I had gone through since *MGS1*. *Metal Gear Solid* came out when we wanted to be much more capable and mentally developed than we actually were, and the haunted mansion aesthetic fit perfectly. Realism was important only to a point—the most essential task for *MGS1*'s environment were to immerse, to mystify, and to scare. The series—and the two young Burches playing it—had yet to grow up. *MGS1* fed our imaginations and attempts at maturity with popcorn politics (the PRESIDENT is involved with a terrorist group that's

---

31   **Ash:** In true Kojima form, he actually managed to turn Johnny's IBS into a plot point.

run by a CLONE and has a PSYCHIC? Politics is CRAZY!) and a scary, unpredictable landscape.

ANTHONY

Here's the thing. All that haunted house shit? That's not really the tone of *Metal Gear Solid*. It's, at best, half the tone. While 50% of the game might be about scary rooms and demonic boss fights and creeping horror, the other fifty percent is about switching controller ports and checking the back of your physical CD case and hearing Colonel Campbell teach a hardened mercenary how to climb a ladder.

More than any other game franchise (with the possible exception of Suda 51's No More Heroes series), *Metal Gear Solid* is tonally defined by its willingness to embrace the fact that, yes, it *is* just a video game, and you *are* just a person thwapping buttons on a hunk of plastic.

Case in point: the encounter with Psycho Mantis that we discussed earlier. Before you meet him, all of the game's ambient score cuts out (accompanied, of course, by Snake asking, "What happened to the music?"). Your footsteps echo across the marble floor on the way to his room. Meryl's voice grows harsh and alien, like she's speaking through a gas mask. Pressing triangle— normally the first-person view button—makes you look through Meryl's eyes rather than your own. Then, she suffers a migraine and starts trying to seduce you.

Something is clearly not right.

Things get even weirder when Mantis finally turns off his optic camouflage and confronts you directly. He says he can read your mind and influence physical reality with telekinesis. He then reads your memory card and comments on what you've played (but only if you've played a Konami game recently),[32] moves your controller by making it rumble, then psychoanalyzes you because you haven't saved enough or were too careful around traps.

Individually, these little goofs aren't all that interesting. Even as a kid, I started laughing the moment Mantis said he was about to demonstrate his telekinesis—he was clearly about to move my controller with the rumble feature, because what the hell other options did he have? Sure, our heads exploded when we had to physically disconnect the controller from the first port and plug it into the second—but we don't love *MGS1*'s fourth wall breaks because they're individually spectacular. We love them because they're a part of the game's basic DNA, an intrinsic part of the logic that keeps the world spinning. When the player needs to

---

32   **Mantis:** "So, you like *SUIKODEN*?!"

know how to perform an action, Colonel Campbell tells Snake the button Snake needs to use.

"Press the action button to drop down."

"Snake, if you want to go up or down a ladder, just press the Action Button by the ladder. Approach the ladder and press the Action Button to climb it."

"Snake, you're under attack from off screen."

Most games make a clear distinction between story dialogue and tutorial dialogue. Story dialogue is supported with voice acting from the main characters. Tutorials sit in a separate room where the characters either don't speak directly to the mechanics, or do so in a weird and indirect way in an attempt to maintain immersion. (In *The Matrix: Path of Neo*, for instance, the designers called the player's special ability "focus" so Trinity and Morpheus can yell, "Neo, just FOCUS," and still technically be giving gameplay advice without breaking the fourth wall.) The player is presented with separate Narrative Stuff and Tutorial Stuff, which they can cleanly and quickly push to different parts of their brain. Oh, the lead actor is talking—this must be Narrative Stuff, so I should be ready to have an emotional reaction. Ah, a text box has popped up on the screen with a big picture of the B button—this is Tutorial Stuff and I need to switch to the part of my brain that focuses solely on figuring out which buttons do what.

Metal Gear Solid does not do this.

Naomi Hunter will discuss the difference between honorable combat and cold-blooded murder with Snake, but five seconds later she'll also ask Snake to put the controller against his arm so she can activate the rumble function and make him feel good. There's no wink and a nod here, no joke to be made. It's a simple, matter-of-fact statement: Snake, I know you're in pain, so just put the controller on your bicep and it'll vibrate.

You'd think that this would result in a horribly distancing, awkward experience. You'd assume that every moment of dramatic weight would be immediately undone by someone using phrases like "Action Button" or "back of your CD case"—that they'd essentially be pulling you back into the real world and reminding you that you're playing a game.

Quite the contrary, this whole-hearted acceptance of the fourth wall's arbitrariness makes *Metal Gear Solid* even more immersive. These little acknowledgements of the player's experience simply create a new tone, a new reality and an engaging new set of diegetic rules. When Naomi massages Snake's arm through the DualShock controller, she's not just doing it to be funny—she's doing it because both Snake and the player have just gotten out of a physically strenuous minigame sequence that required the player to repeatedly hammer the circle button for seconds at a time. She's narratively patching up Snake's wounds, but she's also healing the player's tired arm at the same time.

There's no dissonance here between player and avatar—I feel what Snake feels, and the game responds to both of

43

us. Before the game started intentionally highlighting the player's disconnect from Snake (most notably during Gray Fox's aforementioned sacrifice), I felt like Snake and I were going through the story together. My sense of immersion was never broken because the game redefined what constituted immersion in the first place.

ASH

Which sort of makes me wonder why few other games do this. I know that *Metal Gear Solid* created, broke and then arguably prevented anyone from replicating the mold, but our technology has changed a lot since then, and we haven't really had another game that uses, say, the Kinect or the WiiU pad, to the same effect as *MGS1* does the PlayStation controller. Maybe that's just impossible at this point—maybe only a game as batshit crazy as *Metal Gear Solid* could've gotten away with *that* level of fourth wall breaking. But that sort of feels like saying that no other film could feature a character looking directly into the camera lens after *La Jetée*.[33] [34]

---

33   **Anthony:** Look at *me* I saw a *French* thing I'm *Ashly* do you want to talk about *existential things* and *different types of coffee*.

34   **Ash:** Don't even test me—I can say types of coffee all day. Mocha. Espresso. Ma-macchiato.

ANTHONY

A lot of Metal Gear fans refer to these[35] sorts of moments as Easter eggs. While that classifier might be accurate for other, more self-serious games, it simply doesn't apply to *Metal Gear Solid*. Easter eggs exist outside the normal tone and logic of the game—they're a special, hidden secret. When you enter the Statue of Liberty in *Grand Theft Auto IV* and see a massive, beating heart lashed with chains, that's an Easter egg. When you go through a secret door in *Doom II* and fight John Romero, that's an Easter egg. But what do you call it when a game breaks the fourth wall *all the time*, without bothering to hide it? Even if you skip all the cutscenes and codec conversations in the game, you still *have* to experience Naomi's rumble-centric medical care. You still have to watch your screen go black during the Mantis fight, with only the word "HIDEO" sitting in the corner of the screen, trying to convince you that the game has somehow fiddled with your television's input settings. These are not secret, tonally independent distractions from the main game. These *are* the main game.

There's also a simple novelty to *Metal Gear Solid*'s lack of a fourth wall—it keeps you curious. As the game mashes together horror, drama, romance, and

---

35 **Ash:** Latte.

gags about vibrating controllers, you can't help but wonder: What the fuck is going to happen next? Will someone spend twenty minutes talking about the importance of nuclear disarmament? (Yes.) Is someone then going then suggest that you pour ketchup on yourself to fool a guard into thinking you're dead? (Yes.) During a boss fight with a helicopter, will your colonel ask you to listen for the sound of its rotors if you have a stereo audio setup? If you have a mono setup, will he then shrug sheepishly and say that you can probably still beat the helicopter anyway? (Yes and yes.)

Somehow, Kojima and his team managed to turn *MGS1*'s potpourri of styles and tones into something greater than the sum of its parts. *Metal Gear Solid* doesn't feel like a horror flick *and* a *Naked Gun*-esque comedy *and* an action movie *and* a stealth game. *Metal Gear Solid* feels like *Metal Gear Solid*. It has a style unto itself that I've never seen emulated. I've never even seen a game that's been *compared* to it. I've played dozens of games described as being "*Metroid*-like," or "*Uncharted*-esque," or "*Gears of War*-lite," but I've never played any game that had a tone or style that justified comparison to *Metal Gear Solid*.

You get a sense, for good or ill, that nobody ever told Kojima "no." That any idea, no matter how seemingly dissonant or irrelevant, was ever shot down. And though that may result in the occasional cringeworthy moment, it also gave the world a game that is as inventive as it is inscrutable.

THEMES?

ASH

The Hurt Locker opens with a quote from journalist Chris Hedges that sets up the thematic framework for the rest of the movie: "The rush of a battle is a potent and often lethal addiction, for war is a drug." In the film, our protagonist, William James (played by Jeremy Renner),[36] is the leader of a U.S. Army Explosive Ordinance Disposal unit who has been in and out of combat for most of his adult life. He's lives for the adrenaline rush that only near-death experiences can afford him. And when his rotation ends and he returns to a civilian life, he can only handle what he views as the mundanity of day-to-day life for a few weeks before he throws himself into another tour of duty.

---

36   **Ash:** Or "pseudo-Nathan Fillion" as I like to call him. Even though he's currently better known than Nathan Fillion. Because those who love *Firefly* will be punished.

Metal Gear Solid told nearly the same story a decade earlier.

Replaying the game as an adult, I am—I can't believe I'm saying this—struck by the game's nuanced and oddly elegant treatment of the psychology of soldiers.

Replace "explosives expert" in *The Hurt Locker* with "cyborg ninja" in *Metal Gear Solid* and you essentially have Gray Fox. Gray Fox is a man who, much like Snake, has only known a life of war. All he understands, all he excels at, is killing. So much so that his superiors subjected him to genetic experimentation with the intention of turning him into a super soldier. This experimentation drives him mad, he loses sight of his humanity, and he becomes consumed with the need to fight and kill Snake. Like William James, Gray Fox is a man forged in the fire of war and finds it impossible to escape.

When Gray Fox finally tracks down Snake to fulfill his "destiny" of killing his former comrade, Snake asks Gray Fox why he wants to fight him. "Is it for revenge?"

"It is nothing so trivial as revenge," Fox answers. "A fight to the death with you. Only then will my soul have respite. I will kill you or you will kill me… it makes no difference." Then, when the moment transitions from cutscene to battle, Fox says, "Make me feel it—make me feel alive again!" Once you get him near death, his cyborg skeleton begins to crackle and spark, and he cries that he's been "waiting for this pain!" Every subsequent punch you land is met with a plea from Fox: "Hurt me more!"

So… something's going on here.[37]

You could attribute his insanity to having been toyed with by evil scientists, and you certainly wouldn't be off base. But it's telling that after all the genome experiments, when reduced to just his core being, Gray Fox is defined by a literal lust for battle. Gray Fox *seems* indiscriminately violent—certainly, killing a room full of scientists is a bit excessive—but in his mind, he's simply clearing out all the "obstacles" that stand in the way of him having an honorable fight with his friend and rival, Snake. At his core, he doesn't need senseless violence, he needs war. He needs to be killed in a battle. The pain of a battle with a worthy opponent is the only thing that makes him feel alive anymore.

In terms of the greater narrative, Gray Fox's story essentially serves as a cautionary tale to Snake, who is walking the exact same path, toeing the dangerous line between man and war machine. Gray Fox can be kind and even self-sacrificial, but he's also a cold-blooded murderer. If Gray Fox is sympathetic, it's because his evil comes not from within, but from the reality of his circumstances.

---

37 **Anthony:** Yaaay consensual giving and receiving of pain. Booo it being treated as a thing only emotionally broken people do.

It's significant that Fox comes to Snake for his battle to the death. It's not just that they're friends, it's what Snake represents. Snake is him, before he went insane. Just like Fox, Snake is a soldier. Just like Fox, the only thing he is good at is killing. Just like Fox, Snake has no real family. They are effectively shadows of people, significant only for the destruction they can cause.

But at the end of the game, we see Snake begin to veer from this path. He decides to "choose life," as the game puts it. He tells Meryl[38] he's ready to leave this life behind and start a new one with her. We see the theme begin to break apart a little. Maybe he doesn't *need* war. Maybe he doesn't have to end up like Gray Fox.

Except he kind of does. It's no coincidence that in *MGS4* we learn it was impossible for Snake to settle down and play house with Meryl. Just like Jeremy Renner's character in *The Hurt Locker*, Snake and Fox are tethered to battle and bloodshed. Snake's even more of a misanthrope in *MGS4* than he was in *MGS1*, even less apt at showing emotion or empathizing with those around him. And the way Meryl treats him—with icy indifference at one moment and intense anger the next—it's clear that he was one hell of a shitty partner. Like any addict, his addiction to war is all he has room for.

---

38   **Ash:** If she doesn't die. We'll talk about this a bit later.

When Liquid accuses Snake of "enjoying all the killing," at the end of the game he's speaking to a truth about the player, but also a truth about Snake. He tolerates his dangerous job, but there's a part of him—like Gray Fox—that enjoys it. The surface-level plot is about Snake fighting a band of quirky, esoteric terrorists, but the subtext is Snake's fight against his own nature, against his own genetic branding, against his addiction to war.

ANTHONY

This ties into one of the game's other main themes: that soldiers are treated as nothing more than tools by the people who control them. Gray Fox is the result of scientists trying to turn him into a literal tool: a blending of man and machine that you could just hurl at your enemies while you took cover. Even though Fox sort-of-successfully fights against his fate, he can't run from who he is. He's a deadly, robotic tool of destruction who gets killed by Metal Gear REX—an even deadlier, even more robotic tool of destruction.

Snake doesn't fare much better.

At the end of the game, we find out that Snake was infected with a virus called FOXDIE.[39] From the

---

39   **Ash:** The US government has a flare for the dramatic in the MGS world. And in our world?

government's perspective, the events of the game are nothing but a massive test of FOXDIE's capabilities. Snake is told he needs to rescue two particular hostages, but the government only wanted to get him close enough to infect and kill them. At every turn, Snake is lied to, tricked, and generally fucked over by the bad guys and good guys alike.

Time and time again throughout the series, Snake and Big Boss attempt to exercise their free will only to find themselves at the mercy of higher powers—of the military, of a nefarious illuminati, of a rogue computer AI that went crazy and wants to take over the world through internet memes or something.[40] At nearly no point in any of the Metal Gear games is Snake not being manipulated by some third party. He, like Fox, is a tool. Unlike Fox, he's a consistently useful one.

ASH

MGS1—in another surprising display of thematic aptitude—also taps into the reality of why many people are attracted to the armed services, as evidenced by Meryl's backstory.

A few hours into the game, prompted by Snake's insinuation that she's a rookie who can't handle herself in battle, Meryl describes her personal motivations for

---

40   **Anthony:** *Metal Gear Solid 2* is not a good game.

becoming a soldier. She says that she never knew her father, and that the only information she had about him was that he was a soldier. So she joined the military to learn more about him, which would, she assumed, help her learn more about herself. This vague piece of background information does little to help our understanding of who Meryl is or to make her feel more real. All we know is that she's desperately grasping for meaning.

But the thing is, that's an actual reason people join the military.[41]

That's certainly not why *everyone* does it, but there's a significant number of people in the armed forces who enlisted because they felt that the military provided greater meaning and structure than the other possibilities available to them.

This is an example of Kojima's trickery—his use of established tropes as a shorthand for characterization. It's irrelevant if this parallel between Meryl and real life young soldiers like her was intentional because it's easy for me to draw an immediate correlation between this fictitious character and people I know in real life. I began to fill in the blanks of what she must think and feel because I know how people in a similar position think and feel. You know what your pal Cassie was

---

41   **Anthony:** Also: free haircuts.

going through when she decided to join the military, what motivated her, and what she was hoping to gain from the experience, and it's easy to project that personal context onto Meryl. I feel a twinge of empathy for Meryl—I can imagine that feeling of aimlessness, that desperate search for meaning, that fear of never finding direction of purpose. Suddenly, I'm moved, almost despite myself. And Kojima didn't have to write a single interesting line of dialogue to produce that effect.

That singular piece of Meryl's characterization also speaks to *MGS1*'s overt, screaming-in-your-face, flashing-neon-sign, is-everyone-taking-notes theme: Your genes aren't your fate. This is an idea that's at the core of all the game's main characters. It plays a major role in Snake's and Otacon's arcs, it factors into Meryl's and Naomi's stories, and it's the tenuous justification for why Liquid is a war-mongering psychopath.

Meryl's quest to become a soldier is tied to her father and the sense of identity she thinks that connection can give her. She's chasing the idea of her dad, hoping that following a familial, genetic path will give her a sense of self. Meryl's arc (if you can even call it that) is learning that war is ugly and that there's nothing glamorous about being a soldier.[42] She

---

42   **Ash:** No shit, Meryl.

doesn't mention her father again because why bother wasting any more time characterizing Meryl, but we can infer that by acknowledging that war sucks, she realizes that following in daddy's footsteps to find herself was a pretty bogus idea. The way she "defies her genes" is by finding purpose in her love for Snake. It's a tenuous, underdeveloped iteration of the theme, but *whadayagonnado*. Meryl is a shitty character.

Similarly, Naomi, who doesn't know anything about her biological parents, becomes a genetic scientist for the same reason that Meryl becomes a soldier—to understand who she is. She believes that deciphering her genes will unlock her purpose and meaning. The idea is equally misguided, and Naomi admits as much during a long, obvious monologue at the end of the game.

We get a better sense of the game's main thematic thrust with Otacon. Otacon's arc is fueled by his family's history. He's a genuinely nice guy who becomes an engineer to help people, and is devastated when Snake tells him that his creations are being perverted and transformed into nuclear weapons. He talks of his father, who was a member of the Manhattan Project, and how that legacy haunts him to this day. "We must have the curse of nuclear weapons written into our DNA," Otacon laments, suggesting that creating nuclear weapons is a genetic predisposition, that he's cursed to live the same mistakes his father made.

But in helping Snake destroy his own creation, Otacon defies that trajectory. At the end of his arc in *MGS1*, he has taken responsibility for his life and his work. He breaks the destructive cycle established by the men in his family and proves to himself that his DNA doesn't have to be his destiny.

But the game's best representation of this theme is, predictably, conveyed through Snake and his relationship to Liquid. You couldn't ask for a more on-the-nose, here's-your-theme-you-want-fries-with-that-character pairing than Solid Snake and Liquid Snake. Given that they are clones who have *directly opposing goals and desires*, their existence is a statement of the theme in and of itself. Your genes obviously can't be your destiny if one clone wants to save society from nuclear destruction and the other one wants to instigate nuclear destruction. Liquid is a power-crazy sociopath with the ability to stage elaborate, manipulative, and bafflingly effective plans, whereas Snake is a dense charmer who at least occasionally has the capacity to care for other people. Liquid is also *obsessed* with Big Boss, their "father"—what he did or didn't do, how he treated Liquid, how Liquid sizes up against him—whereas Snake really doesn't care. In fact, Snake kills Big Boss because (a) dude wanted it, and (b) dude needed to die. And, lest we forget,

Liquid has a British accent for no reason. Two clones that could not be more different.

"But, Ashly," you might say, "Liquid and Solid *are* different genetically—one of them got Boss's recessive genes, and the other got his dominant genes."

Astute observation, you precocious upstart. As Liquid states in the first part of his long obligatory villain monologue:

> We're twins linked by cursed genes. Les enfants
> terribles. You're fine. You got all the old man's
> dominant genes. I got all the flawed, recessive
> genes. Everything was done so that you would
> be the greatest of his children. The only reason
> I exist is so they could create you!

So, yes, technically they're not genetically identical.

However, if you stick around after the credits, you hear Ocelot speaking on the phone to someone who is later revealed to be the president of the United States (DUN DUN DUNNNN). In that conversation, Ocelot states that it was actually *Liquid* who had The Boss's dominant genes all along. In fact, Liquid's sense of mediocrity was self-fulfilling prophecy, for he had what would be considered the Boss's "superior" genes the entire time. His *perception* of his genetics and what they meant about him decided his fate, not his actual physical makeup.

Or if you don't want to do all that deduction and analysis, Naomi states the theme outright at the end of the game:

> The most we can say about DNA is that it governs a person's potential strengths... potential destiny. You mustn't allow yourself to be chained to fate... to be ruled by your genes. Humans can choose the type of life they want to live.

HEY DO YOU REMEMBER WHEN ALL THOSE CHARACTERS THOUGHT THEIR GENES WERE THEIR FATE? THEIR GENES WEREN'T ACTUALLY THEIR FATE.

DID YOU—DID YOU GUYS GET THAT?

I assume they spelled out the major theme of the game so that children could understand. I certainly didn't, though, when I was a kid. Naomi's ending monologue flew right over my head. I guess I was just happy that Liquid was finally out of the picture, distracted by the weird stock-footage of buffalo, and diluted her monologue down to "have a good life, Snake—byeeeeeeee."

While I'm surprised at just how much talk of free will I missed as a kid, there's one theme in the game that impacted me and Anthony in a visceral, tangible way.

ANTHONY

Metal Gear Solid was the first game to tell me killing people wasn't cool.

The particular scene I'm thinking of has since become marginally famous amongst the MGS fan community. Partially because it brings some of the series's themes and contradictions into sharp relief, and partially because the phrase "super baby method" is uttered twice in ascending levels of gravel-voicedness.

Snake (shirtless) has been tied down by his twin brother (also shirtless) to talk. To rap. To *get real*.[43] After a brief monologue about genetics and cloning, Liquid stops messing around: "Why are you here, then? Why do you continue to follow your orders while your superiors betray you? Why did you come here? Well, I'll tell you, then—you enjoy all the killing. That's why."

"What?!"

"Are you denying it? Haven't you already killed most of my comrades? [...] I saw your face while you did it. It was filled with the joy of battle. [...] There's a killer inside you—you don't have to deny it."

Reading that exchange today, I'm struck by how cheesy it all is, and how many individual sentences could stand to be cut from each line. Is it that important

---

43   **Anthony:** Real shirtless.

for Liquid to ask, "Why are you here?" and then, "Why did you come here?" a sentence later?

But when I was ten?

That shit blew my *mind*.

I *was* filled with the joy of battle when I killed Liquid's friends. I *did* enjoy all the killing. Even though I tried to play the game stealthily, I took a quiet pleasure in screwing up and getting spotted every so often, just because it gave me an excuse to start tearing baddies apart with my FAMAS machine gun.

A couple of years later, I'd play the noncanonical Metal Gear Solid game for the Game Boy Color (known in Japan as *Metal Gear: Ghost Babel* and then in the West as, confusingly, *Metal Gear Solid*) and find an even more clever implementation of this scene. Instead of just pointing out that Snake murdered the other boss baddies in the game, *Ghost Babel* antagonist Pyro Bison tells you the exact number of enemies you killed in order to reach him.

Even without a body count, Liquid Snake's *MGS1* scene was a revelation. I'd played a fair number of shooters before Ash got her PlayStation, and I enjoyed every one of them.[44] To play a game where the antagonist chastised me for the very thing I enjoyed? How insightful! How provocative!

---

44 **Anthony:** *GoldenEye 007* more so than the others, because slappers only.

Times change, of course.

Thanks to *BioShock*, it's become en vogue to make games about shooting hundreds of people with stories about how awful the player is for pulling the trigger. *Far Cry 3*, *Spec Ops: The Line*, *Hotline Miami*. Action game developers love to play the "you're a monster for doing that thing we made you do" card, and when done poorly, it rings pretty hollow and disrespects the player's intelligence.

Sure, your villain can ask the player why they enjoy killing bad guys, but the answer will always be the same: *Because this is a video game, stupid. Because I can tell the difference between virtual murder and real murder. Because I only had two choices: Either commit the simulated violence you required me to commit in order to see the rest of your condescending story, or stop playing the game altogether. Since I paid money for my game and would like to see how it ends, I will choose to continue playing and suffer your narrative finger-wagging and head-shaking.*

Game developers often include big narrative ideas like this try to bring a game's ludonarrative dissonance—the gulf between the player's actual behavior in gameplay and what the story claims the game is about—into the spotlight and comment on video games/morality/whatever. These games claim narrative depth and wisdom without putting forth any of the actual work, like putting a sprig of parsley on a Big Mac and pretending you've prepared a five-star meal.

If game developers wanted to make a statement about the player's capacity for violence, they wouldn't build a totally normal game with a few lines of half-assed introspective dialogue, they'd bake those concepts into the game mechanics themselves.[45]

But honestly? When you look at the list of anti-violence/pro-violence games out there? *Metal Gear Solid* does a better job of this than most.

Take the game I wrote, *Borderlands 2*, for example. The bad guy, Handsome Jack, refers to the playable characters as "criminals," or "monsters." His reasoning? You kill hundreds of thousands of people and animals in your attempts to reach him and put a bullet in his face. He wants to eradicate all the criminals and save Pandora, but mass-murdering bastards like you make things harder for him. Jack may just be spewing anti-good-guy propaganda like all good baddies should, but we often had friendly characters repeat similar things about you. Even your *friends* think much the same of you that Handsome Jack does.

In one sense, Jack might have a point. You don't just murder thousands of creatures, but you also loot their dead bodies. You're positively *thrilled* to grab a rare gun off the corpse of a Hyperion engineer (whose dying

---

45 **Anthony:** e.g. *Papers Please, XCOM, Crusader Kings II*.

words may well have been, "I only had one week 'til retirement…"), and you won't stop for a second before equipping that gun and melting the faces of a dozen more psychopaths.

But on the other hand: That's all bullshit. You *have* to kill thousands of people because if you don't, you won't earn enough experience points to level up. If you can't level up, you'll lose every single fight. If you lose every single fight, the bad guy will (hypothetically) win and kill all the "bad guys" (anyone who isn't on his side) on Pandora. So, yeah, killing thousands of people might seem like a horrible atrocity out of context, but it's also the only choice that makes any sense in the world and mechanics of *Borderlands 2*.

Contrast that with *Metal Gear Solid*. Liquid says that Snake likes killing people, and that's bad. But since *MGS1* is a game that encourages you to *avoid* people, Liquid's accusations get more interesting.

If you were like me and really *did* enjoy your few chances to commit wanton violence, Liquid's words cut pretty deep. Why did I kill so many people after triggering an alert? Murdered enemies generally don't drop anything of use, so why did I take such pleasure in snapping necks and firing my silenced pistol at unaware guards? I could have just as easily gotten through most of the game without taking a single human life, so *what the hell is wrong with me?*

Granted, Liquid's argument is still a little shaky. You *must* kill a certain number of people to get through the game (the bosses and a few of the enemies during scripted ambush sequences), and the game's plot doesn't change at all depending on how many people you kill. Compared to *Dishonored*, which alters dialogue, the world state, and the ending depending on how much violence the player lets their superpowered hero indulge in, *MGS1* inevitably comes up a little short.

Still, it was the first step on a path that got more morally interesting as it progressed. *MGS2* allowed you to complete the game without killing a single person. *MGS3* tracked every person Snake killed and forced you to confront all of them again in a single paranormal boss fight. *MGS4* allowed you to kill as many people as you wanted, but punished you if you went too insane in a single battle. The punishment? Snake stops fighting, loses a lot of psyche strength, and hears Liquid's words echoing in his head: "*You enjoy all the killing.*"

He also vomits, but that isn't as strong a point to end on.

ASH

As I mentioned, I didn't pick up on many of *MGS1*'s themes when I was a kid. But, much like Anthony, the idea that murder is bad was the one thematic thread that really stuck with me. Why did that one hit home, of all the themes the game presents? It's not like it was particularly subtle, but, again, the "genetics are not your destiny" theme was repeatedly beating me over the head and it never made it through my thick skull. The difference?

Kojima used the tools of his medium to convey one theme and not the other.

I was the one killing the soldiers. *I* was the murderer. I could measure the weight of the killing because I was the one who got to choose whether or not I pulled the trigger. No game has gotten the you-enjoy-all-the-killing theme quite right yet, but *Metal Gear Solid* makes a thematic connection through player choice and interactivity.

The we-are-not-bound-by-our-genes theme is simply delivered through dialogue. Usually in long, drawn-out scenes. These moments don't utilize the strength of the medium—they don't put me into situations where I am forced to confront my own free will. Thus, it was easy for my eight-year-old monkey brain to gloss over it. If you're exploring a theme in your game, using the strengths of the medium to explore that theme will make it resonate much more.

Which is why *Angry Birds* is such an interesting and nuanced exploration of the abuses of the federally subsidized farming systems in the United States.

Just kidding. It's actually about apartheid.

TACTICAL ESPIONAGE ACTION?

MGS1'S STEALTH MECHANICS ARE WEIRD AND NOT VERY GOOD

ANTHONY

For a game that was so transformative for so many gamers, many of *Metal Gear Solid*'s design decisions are just plain *weird*.

Take, for instance, the footprint mechanic. Early on, the game teaches you that if you walk around in the snow, guards will spot your footprints and eventually follow them to your location. This was, and remains, a cool mechanic. It keeps things tense by allowing guards you've bypassed to still track you down, and it allows players to set traps by carefully drawing out a footprint path they want the suspicious guard to follow. Before replaying the game, I looked back at the footprint mechanic with a warm feeling in my stomach: *Ah*, I said. *What an incredibly innovative, multifaceted little idea. It was* Metal Gear Solid*'s deep exploration of mechanics like that which have made it last so long.*

Here is a list of every location in the game where the footprint mechanic is used:

- The helipad level at the beginning of the game

Kojima's team built the footprint mechanic, coded the AI to be interested in the footprints in a particular way, made art for the footprints, created special animations for the guards to use when they follow said footprints, made a tutorial level to teach the player how to use and abuse the footprint mechanic, and then only used that mechanic once in the entire game what the *fuck*.[46]

And it's at the beginning of the game! It's one of the game's more complex stealth systems and it shows up before you've even had a chance to understand the vision cones. The footprints could have easily been introduced later on.

I worked at a game development studio for three years, and if a designer ever went to a producer and

<hr>

46   **Anthony:** Kojima!

suggested spending *that* much manpower on a mechanic the designer only planned to use once, that would be the easiest conversation of the producer's professional life.

Sure, the footprint mechanic saw a lot of use in the expansion/sort-of-sequel *Metal Gear Solid: VR Missions*—not that Kojima could have been certain *Metal Gear Solid* would be popular enough to justify the expansion treatment—but who the hell designs an entire stealth system based around enemies following footprints in the snow and then sets 95% of their game indoors?

Probably the same sort of designer who creates tons of mechanics and then forgets to make them interact in worthwhile ways.

•

I used to think about *Metal Gear Solid* the same way I currently think about great immersive sims like *Thief, Deus Ex,* and *Dishonored*.[47] Those games were so built on player agency that play styles and strategies often

---

47   **Anthony:** For the uninitiated, the "immersive sim" is a game genre originating with *Ultima Underworld* in 1992. Immersive sims focus on—wait for it—immersion. They provide compelling, consistent game worlds. They give the player many different options with which to complete their goals. They include numerous overlapping game systems that result in emergent storytelling. It also so happens that many of the greatest immersive sims are stealth games, but not all stealth games are immersive sims.

emerged that the designers hadn't even thought of. *Dishonored*'s deep and interconnected systems, for instance, might allow players to take several disparate mechanics like the following:

- The player can put remote mines onto things
- The player can create rats out of thin air
- The player can psychically possess a rat

…and combine them into a remarkably clever means of assassinating a target. Because the player is smart, and because the mechanics are universal and interconnected, the player can summon a rat, place a remote mine on its back, then possess the rat and command it to walk up to the assassination target so the remote mine explodes and completes the mission.[48] This is the sort of design philosophy that makes so many immersive sims like *Splinter Cell*, *Mark of the Ninja*, or *Monaco* work as well as they do.

Despite its honorary title as the father of the modern stealth game, *Metal Gear Solid* is about as far from the immersive sim genre as you can possibly get.

Though *MGS1* gives the player 29 tools to use (nineteen items and ten weapons), most of those tools don't synergize well with other items. What's the C4

---

48   **Ash:** Poor little guys.

do? It blows people up and hurts them while alerting everyone. What's the stun grenade do? It knocks every single person out. What's the chaff grenade do? It knocks every single camera out. Where a good stealth game encourages the player to use their tools in combination with one another to solve problems (like, say, using a noisemaker to lure a guard into a trap in *Mark of the Ninja*), *MGS1*'s tools are too shallow to be used for anything other than their most basic purpose. They're less like interesting tools to be used in creative ways and more like different keys on a big-ass keyring. Oh, there's a bunch of cameras in that corridor? Let me just find my chaff grenade key to solve that problem with zero fuss.

ASH

I agree with what you're saying, but I derived an odd comfort from the linearity in *MGS1* because stealth games are terrifying to me. I spent most of *Deus Ex* running and screaming. Knowing that I have a magical bullet for certain situations gave my heart a break. I wonder if that was part of the justification? Kojima seemed to want *MGS1* to be a cinematic experience first and foremost (which is weird, because he was making a video game), and if the stealth was too hard, it would've barred more people from enjoying the story he was crafting.

ANTHONY

This gets into a different discussion about story fighting gameplay in terms of accessibility (I think every game should have a story-only mode where you can't die), but I see what you're getting at.

The player is encouraged to be clever, but in a linear way—the game is made up of puzzles to be solved, rather than scenarios to be experimented with. A couple of the puzzles have more than one solution, sure, but even these moments are fairly shallow, offering a choice of several one-dimensional solutions rather than options of real depth. When facing the guards at the end of the long bridge preceding the Hind D fight, for instance, you can either snipe them, fire missiles at them, or toss a stun grenade. There's no interesting back-and-forth, no planning or improvisation—just three equally valid and simple answers in a multiple choice test.

MGS1 does a great job of teaching the player one simple lesson from which all the other mechanics follow: Whatever happens, do *not* trigger an alert. Alert mode causes more enemies to spawn with more thorough patrol patterns, and since these special alerted enemies don't drop much (if any) loot when they die, the player gains nothing by putting the base on alert other than the likelihood of a quick death and the promise of hearing Snake's name three more times. Sure, the alert will expire after a few minutes if you manage to hide

(Shadow Moses's genetically enhanced super soldiers have the memory of goldfish), but there's still no upside to triggering an alert.

While *MGS1* should be commended for attempting to make alerts as terrifying for the player as possible, the AI's propensity to go on alert at every gunshot or explosion—and the fact that the alert state is universal rather than local—means that a lot of potentially interesting strategies are simply not valid.

For instance, I *could* set down a proximity mine and then lure an enemy over to it by making noise, but once he hits the mine it'll explode loudly enough that everyone in the area will probably go on alert anyway. Hell, even if he happened to be far enough away that the other guards don't hear it, then why even bother spending the claymore? Better to just *hurk-hurk-hurk-hurk-snap-ahh* him from behind and save yourself the trouble. Want to use a non-silenced gun to take out a distant enemy? The base will go on alert. Want to plant a remote C4 charge in an enemy's patrol pattern and detonate it right when he walks over it? Assuming anyone else is even remotely nearby: Alert. Accidentally hit the "fire" button while wielding nearly any gun?[49] Alert, alert, alert.

---

49   **Ash:** Read: *what I did all the time.* Anxious trigger finger. I wouldn't recommend ever putting me in a firefight situation.

Quite simply, the alert state is too hellishly punishing and easily triggered to allow the player any truly creative ways to progress through most levels. Is it more "realistic?" Sure, I guess—as realistic as you can be in a game about supervillains stealing a giant robot. Does it make the game less fun? Unquestionably.

•

On paper, *MGS1*'s stealth system is great. It's clear, it's readable, it's intuitive.

All guards have vision cones. If the player steps into that vision cone, the guard gets alerted. If the player makes a noise or does something odd from a distance, the guard gets curious and tries to get you into their vision cone so they can then get alerted.

Simple.

Snake's radar makes the enemy's vision cones clear, and therefore you always know exactly how a guard managed to spot you. Clarity of consequence is essential to stealth game design—it's why Sam Fisher and Garrett both arbitrarily own magical items which tell them how dark the shadow they're standing in is—so this clean, readable visual feedback is wonderfully useful.

Of course, one could make the argument that it's *too* useful. When playing *MGS1*, it's incredibly easy to focus on the radar at the exclusion of nearly everything else in the game. The minimap includes almost all of the information you could possibly need, from guards, to cameras to doors. Why bother watching an enemy's idle animations to get a clue about which direction he might turn once he starts moving again? Why bother looking around corners? The top-down radar tells you *everything* you need to know. Often, it's not hard to feel like you're just playing *Pac-Man*… except slower-paced and with worse controls.

THE CONTROLS ARE A BOSS FIGHT

ANTHONY

None of the Metal Gear Solid games controlled better than a horse-drawn buggy trapped in a swamp made of fresh boogers. (Until *Metal Gear Solid 4*, at least.)

To reload Snake's gun in *MGS1*, you need to unequip it, then equip it again. To use an item, you need to use it *while* the item menu is open. Did you accidentally equip the item? You—you *idiot*. You stupid *idiot*. You can't *use* items you've equipped. Oh, and do you want to fire your gun while moving? Just press the weapon button, then press the crouch (what) button while keeping the weapon button held. Then, if you want to fire the weapon as you run around like a confused toddler, you *release* the weapon button (what) and pray that your spray of bullets hits something because the weapon auto-aim only works when your character is stationary.

Granted, there aren't many instances in which you'd *want* to fire while moving. The camera is so close to Snake that most enemies you shoot are likely outside the boundaries of your screen.

I shot my way through most of my first playthrough by taking advantage of the fact that Snake's auto-aim distance starts working farther than his view distance. If you know an enemy is somewhere to the north of your current screen, you can just take out your silenced SOCOM pistol, press the weapon button, and wait to see if the auto-aim locks onto your target. Then just quickly tap the weapon button three or four times, and *piff-AHH-piff-AHH-piff-AHHOUhGHGHHHGHh*, the bad guy will go down without you even having *seen* him. For a stealth-action game, this is poor design.

The Ocelot fight, which sees you navigating the perimeter of a square room while shooting across its trip-mine-filled center, is spectacularly suspenseful... often for the wrong reasons. If you accidentally touch the center of the room, you fail. If you accidentally shoot the hostage in the center of the room too many times, you fail. This is the first boss fight of the game, and it puts you on the edge of annihilation from the word "draw." It's a well-constructed enemy encounter whose only sin is highlighting the deficiencies of the control scheme. Because Ocelot constantly moves around the room's perimeter and takes cover behind impenetrable pillars, most players will adopt one of two strategies to beat him.

In the first strategy, you'll stay in one place and aim at Ocelot, hoping you can catch him with auto-aim before he ricochets a bullet into your face and stuns you. When he moves, you have to move (but not *too* far) and repeat the process. The boss fight becomes a sort of ballet, if ballet consisted of dancers moving two feet, stopping abruptly, moving another two feet, stopping abruptly, and then shooting each other in the face.

In the second strategy, you chase Ocelot with your gun drawn, shoot him point-blank in the back of the head, and wait for him to stop flickering (*MGS1* was, after all, a game of the 90s) so you can do it again… assuming you don't accidentally run into the tripwired explosives while holding down roughly a third of the buttons on the controller.

Generally, boss fights are meant to be a culmination of every lesson the player learned in the game so far. Because it forces the player to wrestle with the already-awkward controls in a situation where a single misstep will lead to failure, the Ocelot boss fight is an oddly appropriate final exam. The preceding levels taught the player that aiming, shooting, and running are awkward and difficult interactions; the Ocelot fight acts as a gate where the player must prove that they can handle the inelegant controls to do something delicate. If they can't, the rest of the game will be an absolute *nightmare*.

Most of the *Metal Gear Solid* boss fights work like this—they're struggles with the controls rather than with the antagonist.

Both Sniper Wolf fights are difficult not because Wolf is hard to spot, but because when she shoots you while you have a sniper rifle equipped, Snake flinches and his aim goes so crazy that the quickest way to put your crosshairs back where you were looking is to unequip the sniper rifle, maneuver Snake's crawling body so he's kinda-sorta looking in the direction you last remember aiming at Wolf, equip the sniper rifle again, then wander around with the crosshair until you see something that looks familiar.

The tank fight against Vulcan Raven flummoxes *MGS1* speedrunners to this day. The movement of the tank, the timing of the grenade, and the relationship between how long you hold down the weapon button and how far the grenade flies when you finally release it are so random and bizarre that a talented player who can easily breeze through the rest of the game without even stopping for a breath will waste entire minutes trying to land the grenade in *juuuuust* the right spot to damage Raven's tank gunner.

Only the simplest fights such as the Metal Gear REX duel (shoot this thing in the face with a missile), the Hind D duel (shoot this thing in the cockpit with a missile), and the Liquid Snake fistfight (punch this thing in the face with a punch) manage to avoid the poor controls and put the challenge where it should be.

THE MOST FUN PART OF THE GAME?

ANTHONY

The second time you meet Raven,[50] he's left the protection of his armored tank and fights you, shirtless and grunting, in a big-ass freezer. The frozen arena you fight in is a grid of intersecting horizontal and vertical pathways separated by evenly distributed metal containers. As Raven stalks around the room trying to get you into his vision cone so he can tear you to ribbons with his minigun, it's up to the player to find a way to kill Raven that doesn't involve direct combat (because his minigun will obliterate you before you can

---

50   **Raven:** "Sneks don beelong een Ahlasska."

get much of a shot off) or shooting him in the back (because his massive ammo backpack shields him from all rear attacks). For the first and only time in the game, the player has a *ton* of options for how to deal with Raven that don't come down to simple Coke-or-Pepsi choices.

You can set claymore or C4 traps and try to lure him into them. You can sneakily pilot a remote-controlled Nikita missile into his back. You can keep your distance and fire a Stinger missile directly at him before he can lock onto you with his machine gun. Whatever you try to do, Raven continues to patrol the battlefield, knocking some of the teetering metal boxes into the arena and subsequently closing off more of your escape and attack routes. Because Raven is susceptible to so many different types of damage, and because he tears the arena apart as the fight progresses, the player is encouraged to not rely on a single tactic over and over. You must keep moving, keep trying new methods of attack, and keep improvising, all while staying out of Raven's view. (Unless, of course, you *want* him to see you, which can be a useful means of baiting him into a bunch of claymore mines.)

The Raven fight combines all of *MGS1*'s myriad systems into a tense and nonlinear encounter that still withstands the test of time.

ASH

And even though you have many avenues you can take to defeat Raven, the tension and fear of that fight isn't at all diminished. Just because I can fire a rocket at Raven *or* blast him with C4 doesn't change the fact that a HULK-SIZED DUDE CHARGING AT YOU DOWN A NARROW CORRIDOR is scary. Even though you have the power of your full arsenal at your disposal, you feel *just* the right amount of powerless.

ANTHONY

It's also true that other boss fights allow you some choice in how to complete them. The Ocelot gunfight can be won without firing a single shot. If you place a bunch of C4 far enough away from the hostage, you can lure Ocelot into an explosive trap and kill him that way. And when fighting Gray Fox, you can, instead of fighting hand-to-hand as the game clearly wants you to, toss chaff grenades and shoot Fox in the face while he's disabled. (You'll never have enough chaff for the entire fight, though, so the fight will eventually result in the same homoerotic fisticuffs the rest of us experienced.)

And yet, none of these fights are as deep or effectively married to the stealth gameplay as the second Raven fight. Its systems inform and play off one another in interesting ways. According to game designer Robert

Yang, much of the fun in immersive sims comes from "exploiting [interlocking] systems or getting caught unaware by them." When you can see the points where the systems connect and then use those connections to your advantage (or, more hilariously, ignore them to your detriment), you get something deeper and more interesting than those systems would have been in isolation.

Take the second Sniper Wolf boss battle. Even though there are three options for victory, there's no mechanical overlap in this fight. While Sniper Wolf is susceptible to *more* types of damage than Raven (Wolf can be harmed by bullets while Raven can only be harmed by explosives), her positioning in the map forbids the player from engaging with her in anything but the most shallow of ways. The two most interesting things about the Raven fight—positioning and hiding—are absent from the Sniper Wolf fight. This drastically limits the number of ways to deal with her. You can't engage in the kind of violent combinatorics that made up the Raven fight because you simply don't need to. The game design asks you to kill Sniper Wolf from long range, which means you can't use 95% of your arsenal.

To be fair, it's not like this comes as a disappointment—her name's not Close Quarters Combat Wolf. Kojima felt it'd be more fun to try and simulate a sniper duel, however linear and shallow that duel might be, rather than allow the player the same amount of personal expression and strategy they were given during the Raven fight.

The Sniper Wolf fight is fun, sure. It's tense, cinematic. But it doesn't allow for the kind of real creative play the Raven fight does. As a kid—a kid who loved cutscenes and epic music and Call of Duty games—that meant I loved the Sniper Wolf fight more. As an adult, I side with the Raven fight.

ROLLERCOASTERS

ANTHONY

Linear story and gameplay often fight one another. Story is about giving your audience an authored experience designed to evoke a particular reaction: Watch this, be surprised by this, cry at this. Gameplay, conversely, is about allowing the player to make their own decisions: Choose *how* to move your troops, choose *when* to grab a powerup, choose *where* to place that L-shaped *Tetris* block, choose *which* of those cereal boxes in *Gone Home* you'd like to pick up and rotate and toss on the floor to find out whether your sister is a lesbian or not.[51]

---

51   **Anthony:** Gaynor!

The Sniper Wolf fight, like much of *MGS1*, isn't designed to afford the player meaningful choices—it's more about making the player feel as if they're in the middle of a blockbuster action movie. These moments are rollercoaster rides where you can do only a limited number of things. If you do those things, you'll feel awesome and immersed. If you try to color outside the lines, the game will slap you in the face and tell you to start the section over—except this time, *follow directions*. Indeed, if you play the Sniper Wolf fight like an obedient player and whip out your PSG-1, you'll experience a fun (if, again, frustratingly controlled), boss fight where you'll find yourself desperately scanning the landscape for any sign of Wolf or her laser scope. This blockbuster moment is suspenseful and fun, despite (or perhaps because of) the fact that it has almost nothing to do with you or your own personal choices.

The staircase ambush sequence from the middle of the game might be an even better example of this sort of setpiece-driven game design. Upon entering one of the communication towers, an alarm goes off and Snake has to climb *27* flights of stairs while an infinite number of soldiers spawn at Snake's front and rear. This sequence doesn't seem designed to give the player an interesting challenge to overcome. Your only two viable options are "run and shoot a lot" or "keep throwing stun grenades," both of which quickly become tedious. If anything, the scene seems to exist for more pacing and narrative-driven purposes. As you've just escaped a long and relatively action-free bout of imprisonment at the hands of Revolver Ocelot, the game chooses this moment to suddenly and hilariously amp up the action. Did you miss fighting dudes and hearing the alert music? Well then, how would you like to fight *infinity* dudes? With an alert that will *never go away*? Right before rappelling off the *same building you just climbed* while a *helicopter* shoots at you?

It's easy to think of *MGS1* as being a nonstop stealth smorgasbord,[52] but a surprisingly large percentage of the game consists of *Call of Duty*-esque scripted action sequences rather than thoughtful, player-driven stealth.

Just as *Modern Warfare* consisted of The Sniping Level followed by The Level That Takes Place In Total Darkness Forcing You To Use Your Night-Vision Goggles, and The Level Where You're On A Moving Truck Shooting At Things With A Stationary Machine Gun, *MGS1* uses comparatively brief stealth encounters to break up its major action setpieces like The Gas-Filled Tripwire Room or The Level Where You Punch Your Shirtless Brother A Bunch Of Times.

---

52 **Anthony:** *Stealthgasbord*, n: All the stealth you can eat. Typically served lukewarm, under a sneeze guard.

Stealth only occupies the spaces between these linear blockbuster scenes. Stealth is the mortar connecting *MGS1*'s bricks.[53]

On one hand, it was this structure that entranced me as a kid. I never knew what was around the corner either narratively or mechanically. Five seconds ago I was chasing a bunch of rats through an air vent and now I'm shooting a remote-controlled rocket at an electrical box.

On the other hand, this design flies in the face of everything I enjoy as an adult and a game developer. Some of my favorite games—the games I recommend to non-gamers as exemplars of the form—take a set of core mechanics and fully explore them. For example, *Portal* asks a single question—"What if you could put two connected portals on any surface?"[54]—and then spends the game answering that question as fully and as interestingly as it can. It doesn't shy away from exploring the consequences of its own mechanics, and constantly seeks to surprise and excite the player by putting the portal mechanic in new contexts that force the player to think about portals in a new way.

Thief 2: The Metal Age—arguably the greatest stealth game ever made—espouses this same sort of design, but

---

53   **Anthony:** The bricks explode, also.

54   **Ash:** Also: What if a robot was real mean to you all the time?

with sneaking around instead of leaping through portals. Every level explores a different aspect of the game's central stealth systems and asks different questions of the player. What if you had to spend water arrows to kill robotic enemies rather than douse torches?[55] What if you had to return to one centralized area every time you wanted to rob a new room? What if you had to follow someone at night without alerting or harming them?

When I play games like *Portal* or *Thief*, I imagine the designers as Renaissance scientists wearing frilly coats. They're holding some magical artifact of game design in their hands—a heavy, golden, mysterious orb. They raise it up to a candle, they put it under a microscope, they turn it around in their hands, they examine it from every angle. Once they finally understand it, they hand it over to me—in this metaphor I am wide-eyed and eight years old, but not wearing a frilly coat because I am but a peasant—and teach me how to use it.

MGS1, by contrast, spends about twenty seconds looking at its magical artifact before tossing it out a window and cackling, "In the next level, you will have to memorize what a girl's *butt* looks like!"

Because that is a thing you do in *Metal Gear Solid*. That's an *actual thing you do*.

---

55   **Ash:** I often ask that.

Even if you ignore the long cutscenes and codec conversations, *MGS1* is still a linear, narrative-driven rollercoaster ride with lots of weird (often butt-related) twists and turns. If you play along and do as you're asked, exhilaration will follow. If you don't, you'll die. This sort of design implicitly shows the designer's fear that the player might get bored of exploring the game's basic systems, or, even worse, that the game's systems aren't rich enough to justify that kind of exploration in the first place.

That didn't stop me from loving it, of course.

A SLAVE OBEYS

ANTHONY

MGS1 was my absolute favorite game as a child, linearity be damned. Not just that, but it was the first game to teach me that video games—yes, *video games*, those simplistic things I'd been addicted to since my earliest memory of receiving an NES and the *Super Mario Bros./Duck Hunt* combo cartridge—were capable of telling truly interesting stories. Of eliciting actual, emotional reactions from me.

After I finished *Metal Gear Solid*, it became my new high watermark for how video games told stories. I stopped skipping cutscenes. I paid attention to the dialogue in any game I played. If your game wasn't trying to tell an epic, dramatic story, I wasn't interested.

A year later, I'd play *Half-Life*, which felt so clever and fresh in its refusal to ever leave Gordon Freeman's perspective. *Metal Gear Solid* was still great, but it conveyed all of its narrative *oomph* through non-interactive cutscenes. Cutscenes broke immersion, and immersion was now the most important thing in the world. Tell me an interesting and dramatic story, but do it while keeping me immersed.

Next, I stumbled onto *Shadow of the Colossus*. With its minimalistic story and its emotionally charged mechanics, it became my new ideal game. Sure, *Metal Gear Solid* and *Half-Life* were cool, but they paled in comparison to the moment in *Shadow of the Colossus* when you realize, without a single line of spoken dialogue, that the things you've done as a player weren't as heroic as you thought. Just as suddenly, dialogue-heavy cinematic narratives were no longer interesting to me.

Then: *BioShock*. However imperfectly, it combined all my favorite things: metaphor-laden game mechanics, a cracking story, and an immersive environment. Not only that, it allowed the player to be clever. You might have taken out a Big Daddy by laying a bunch of tripwires in front of it, but I took *mine* out by placing a dozen proximity mines on a garbage can and telekinesis-ing it at one of those fuckers so he died in one hit. Through my actions, I created my own, unique player stories.

Then *The Sims 3* got rid of everything *but* the player-generated story. I watched a virtual version of myself die alone in a room full of masterpiece novels. His life goal was to write a certain number of Great Literary Works, but he spent so long sitting alone in his writing room that his girlfriend died of old age shortly after he worked up the guts to marry her.[56] Fuck scripted narrative altogether, I thought. It's all about emergent player stories. Interesting, complex game systems. Stories a player can create through gameplay are a hundred times more interesting, artful, and worthy of praise than anything a writer can cram into an Excel sheet.

Where video game narrative is concerned, my tastes have done a 180 since I first laid my hands on *Metal Gear Solid*. I used to think story was more important than gameplay; now I'm certain gameplay is more important than story. Though I loved it with all my heart as a kid, I now disagree with every narrative philosophy *Metal Gear Solid* represents. It prioritizes its authored story above the player's ability to create their own. It relies

---

56 **Anthony:** He then bought an expensive machine that resurrected her as an angry ghost, but that's dumb so I try to pretend that part didn't happen.

on non-interactive cutscenes rather than conveying its meaning through rules and gameplay.

When I was a kid, I could play through the Sniper Wolf fight and truly feel immersed in the moment. My hands shivered with fear and excitement as I tried to line up a shot. I nearly teared up when Otacon brought Wolf her sniper rifle in a cutscene. I jumped when, in that same cutscene, Snake took out his pistol and shot Wolf in the head. I thought to myself, "Man… I'd love to write something as good as that one day."

Today, I skip that cutscene altogether.

I love the narrative beat, but I think, "Why did I have to shoot Wolf? Why did it happen in a cutscene? Why didn't I have to pull the trigger myself? Or, better yet, what if I could have just walked away from her and skipped all that dialogue while also implicitly refusing to put her out of her misery?

To some extent, it appears games journalism has similarly moved on. For example, *Metal Gear Solid*'s boss fights, despite being weird non sequiturs, were generally praised in 1998. Absolute PlayStation International's review concluded that "the big plus is that they are all completely different and require a great deal of thought to defeat."

Fast forward to 2011 and *Deus Ex: Human Revolution*, whose boss fights were nowhere *near* as random and weird as *Metal Gear Solid*'s:

There are boss fights. They are terrible. And they cannot be avoided. The game is so conflicted about this that there's even a Steam achievement for completing it without killing anyone, which apologetically adds that boss fights don't count. Yes they do, guys. Not for the achievement, maybe, but if you want to play stealthily, evasively, or cleverly, there are four times in the game when you just can't. It's completely incongruous with the rest of the game. (Tom Francis,[57] *PC*[58] *Gamer*[59])

Generally speaking, I'd like to believe players and critics are a lot less forgiving of the types of schizophrenic oddities that we either praised or ignored fifteen years ago. I'd like to believe reviewers are getting increasingly tired of scene-driven gameplay that restricts player's freedom. I'd like to say that my own changing opinions of *Metal Gear Solid* are representative of an industry-wide shift away from authored narrative and toward more player-driven experiences.

I *can't* say that, of course, because *Call of Duty* games still make hojillions of dollars, because *Grand Theft Auto* stopped being about open-world gameplay and started

---

57   **Ash:** Preach, T-France.

58   **Anthony:** Stop calling him that.

59   **Ash:** Never.

being about linear missions that auto-fail the player if they so much as try to have an independent thought, because *BioShock Infinite* discarded all of the complex systems that made *BioShock*'s gameplay interesting and few game reviewers seemed to notice. Is *MGS1*'s mechanical linearity a relic, or an old habit that just won't die? I don't know.

CHARACTERIZATION?

SNIPER WOLF & OTACON

ANTHONY

Given that Solid Snake is the hero of the Metal Gear series, it isn't particularly surprising that we players get attached to him. What *is* surprising is that much of the rest of the cast manages to come off just as round, interesting, and sympathetic as Snake himself.

In *MGS1,* Kojima is particularly adept at making you quickly understand what a character is about. Liquid's FOXHOUND[60] baddies are the best group of bosses in the Metal Gear series. They combine immediately obvious character hooks with surprising depth.

Even Sniper Wolf, who initially seems like your typical femme fatale with plunging cleavage, is more than meets the eye. Like many of the other enemies,

---

60   **Anthony:** Don't worry, it's not an acronym for anything.

she follows a strict moral code and refuses to kill anyone other than her quarry (most notably Meryl, whom she wounds but doesn't execute). She also takes care of her pet wolves as if they were her own children and, as Otacon says, Wolf can't be that bad if she loves animals, right?

So when it's time for Sniper Wolf to die, it's heartbreaking. When Snake mortally wounds Wolf during their second sniper battle, both Wolf and Otacon get a few great moments of characterization. As Wolf lays lungshot on the frozen snow, she launches into a now-typical deathbed monologue that humanizes her and, quite suddenly, makes the player feel bad for shooting her a half-dozen times with a high-powered rifle. The Iraqi government killed Wolf's family and brainwashed her into becoming a soldier. She joined up with Big Boss to get revenge, but now realizes that the revenge turned her into something feral and wrong: "nothing more than a dog." Ever since she first took up arms, she's just been waiting for someone to end her pain.

So far, so schmaltzy.

Until Otacon shows up and falls to his knees with grief. "Why? Why?! I loved you." Wolf reaches out to him, and for a moment, we think that maybe Otacon was right after all. Maybe she does have a heart, and reciprocated Otacon's love.

"My gun," she says, pointing at the rifle at Otacon's feet. "Give it to me." Otacon dutifully places the gun in her arms, and we begin to hear the mournful howling of wolves in the background.

"Okay, hero. Set me free."

Otacon turns away and covers his ears. Snake pulls out his pistol and fires a single shot into Wolf's head.

She never speaks to Otacon during her entire death scene.

Were Otacon's feelings misplaced? Wolf doesn't seem to give a rat's ass about him beyond his ability to bring her the gun, but she also states that she's ready to die because "everyone's here now."

I can't say one way or another whether Wolf was a kind person or not. Before her death, Otacon frequently refers to how nice Wolf was to him and her puppies— that she was a professional above all else, but that she still had a heart. Was she putting on an act? Did Otacon have Stockholm Syndrome mixed with puppy love? Or was she really all those things he said?

ASH

However, the unfortunate thing about Wolf is how she's characterized leading up to and immediately following her moment of reflection and remorse.

A highly sexual, dominatrix-esque villain, she tells you that until she kills you, she's going to be obsessing about you every waking moment. And, according to Ocelot, she might even fall in love with you before she does you in.[61] In all of the following cutscenes that she's featured in, Wolf spends most of her time demanding that she be the one who gets to put Snake in the ground. "He is my target, mine alone," she says, while drawing a heart around a sketch she did of Snake during her lunch break.

Fast forward to you shooting her lung out, and suddenly you're the messiah. She tells you that she's been waiting for a man like you to kill her, and calls you a hero several times before you deliver the final blow.

Sniper Wolf is the most sexualized woman in the game, and is also the only woman who holds any power over Snake. Even though Snake loves Meryl, she's a way of illustrating his power while never actually challenging it. *MGS1* sides with the time-honored idea that sexuality is the only source of female power. Well, in this case, it's sexuality and a high-powered sniper rifle, but female sexuality and death are inextricably linked in the form of Sniper Wolf.

Wolf's entire character is wrapped up in obsession with Snake, to the point that she can't even die without his assistance. She says herself that Snake will be the only thought that occupies her mind until she plugs his

---

61   **Ash:** Maybe Otacon would've gotten more play if he was an assassination target.

nostril with a bullet. I'm pretty sure Raven and Mantis had, like, other things to do. Of course, an assassin becoming obsessed with their target isn't an uncommon trope in fiction. But Wolf being a female assassin colors the nature of the obsession. It perpetuates an inaccurate and destructive stereotype of women as crazy, clingy, and obsessive, and adds to the pantheon of female antagonists who are both obsessive and murderous (e.g. *Swimfan*, *Misery*, *Fatal Attraction*). If Wolf was simply obsessed with killing Snake, that would be consistent with a non-gender specific trope of Assassins in Fiction. But it's that obsession's connection with love and sexuality that causes it to spill into an unfortunate class of female stereotype.

ANTHONY

I interpret Wolf differently. The swimfans and Glenn Closes of the film world derive their violence from an obsession with, and inability to possess and/or gain the approval of, the male protagonist. They're insecure and feel ignored, so they lash out hysterically. Conversely, Wolf is fully in control of her emotions—she just really gets off on murdering. As you referenced, Ocelot says, "sometimes she even falls in love with them before she kills them." I think she's more aroused by the act of killing than the victims themselves.

ASH

The sort of trope presented in *Swimfan* may not be a perfect comparison—but I think the fact that it's implied that Wolf falls in love with Snake means that the lust for killing is an entryway to a complicated, romantic obsession with her target. It's almost like Wolf becomes a dark version of Meryl—Snake becomes Wolf's primary motivation, not just because he's her target, but because of twisted, misplaced love.

Worse still, her death bolsters Snake's status as a heroic figure. It has nothing to do with her, even though she's the one dying. "Okay, hero… set me free" are her last words. *She uses her dying breath to characterize Snake.* And when losing Sniper Wolf is what forces Otacon to take responsibility for his life and his future, she made two dudes' narratives interesting before she kicked the bucket.

The death, kidnapping, torture, and general shitty treatment of female characters is often the impetus for a male's quest, in culture and particularly in video games. It's a tired narrative trajectory, recycled hundreds and hundreds of times, that places men at the center of a story and casts women as either peripheral or invisible. Which isn't to say that female suffering and death are inherently sexist or untouchable as a subject. But the women in *MGS1* tend to suffer to further the narratives of the men around them—not their own.

ANTHONY

It may not bode well for *MGS1*'s feminist credentials that one of its more interesting female characters is made deeper by the actions of a more narratively important male character, but Otacon's crush nonetheless humanizes Sniper Wolf as much as it does him. Though we're told Wolf is sweet in much the same way we were told The Boss mattered to Snake, the characterization is filtered through Otacon's naivete and thus becomes less obvious than *MGS3*'s attempts to make us care about The Boss. Ultimately, regardless of whether or not Wolf is actually worthy of Otacon's love, Otacon's pain is real, and that's worth a hell of a lot.

ASH

Otacon is one of the more interesting, atypical male characters in video games.

So much of gaming is wrapped in male power fantasy. *I'm the strongest dude, I'm the only one who can save the world, I'm stoic and powerful and ain't afraid of nothin'.* Otacon, on the other hand, is none of those things. He's a scared nerd. He doesn't even remotely exist in the same orbit as your Max Paynes, Kratoses, or Snakes. According to the game's logic, the fact that he's emotional—and quite open about those emotions—puts him in a lower social ranking than macho-man Solid Snake.

When you meet him, he immediately pees his pants in fear at the sight of the cyborg ninja, Gray Fox, and soon after he tells you that he's super into robot anime. That's his introduction to the MGS series—urine and robots. In fact, he's so into robot anime that he decides to become an engineer in order to build mechs like the ones in his favorite shows. His nerdiness and initial cowardice are obviously meant to differentiate him from Snake—and we are encouraged to laugh at him when he pisses himself.[62]

But even if the intent of that scene is to make you think Otacon is a dope, the rest of the game challenges that notion. The first challenge comes in the form of his name. Predictably, Otacon wasn't what his mama christened him—his real name is Hal Emmerich. He chooses Otacon as his handle because it originates from the word "otaku," a term used to describe someone obsessed with Japanese culture. And that's what he's known as for the rest of the franchise. His name isn't a hardboiled reference or a generic title—he literally chose it because he's a nerd. And he explains his preference for the name to Snake without a modicum of embarrassment. Despite his cowardice, Otacon is refreshingly confident and unapologetic about who he is. He doesn't see anything wrong with his geekiness (which is nice to see because

---

62   **Ash:** Kojima loves giving lower-social status, comic relief characters uncontrollable bowels, as evidenced by Johnny in *MGS4*.

there *isn't* anything wrong with that), and he conveys that to Snake with almost childlike matter-of-factness. He also emotes openly, which inherently makes him stand out from the pack of most video game characters. There's no instinct in Otacon that makes him "man up" or act tough—if he's scared, he's scared.

And if he's in love, he's in love. From an outsider perspective, it's pretty obvious that the Sniper Wolf/Otacon romance wouldn't happen anywhere outside of fanfiction. She's a vaguely sociopathic, psychologically scarred soldier, and he's a sensitive, emotional man. But that doesn't matter to Otacon—he's an idealist. He believes he and Wolf could be together. And when he mourns her death, it's *moving*. "I couldn't protect her," Otacon says with an unbearable degree of regret. Little Ashly knew that Wolf didn't love him back, but Otacon's sadness was so genuine and earnest that it was heartbreaking. It was enough to make me forget that she almost killed Meryl. I wanted her to live for Otacon.

There are a variety of understandable reasons for Otacon to throw in the towel, but instead he gets the job done. And not *despite* his emotions. He doesn't push his feelings down so he can Be A Man. Helping Snake is his form of mourning, his form of atonement. He openly cries after Snake shoots Sniper Wolf, but not a minute later tells Snake, "I'll hold onto my codec. I want to keep helping." For contrast, Snake's response to Sniper

Wolf's death is to put a handkerchief on her face and say, "I don't have any more tears to shed." COOL. Way to minimize Otacon's emotions and make Wolf's death about you. We get it—you're hardened and stoic—it's very impressive.

Unlike Snake, Otacon's emotions are treated as a motivator, not an inhibitor. He becomes a stronger, more capable person, not by aping Snake or shirking his emotional context, but by leaning into it. Turns out you can be heroic and strong without sacrificing every character trait that makes you an emotionally healthy human.

It's no wonder that Otacon is universally loved. He feels like a real person. Fans of the Metal Gear series don't look down on him for being weak or nerdy. Quite the opposite—it makes him sympathetic and endearing. He's a great guy with the worst fucking luck. But despite that, he carries on. He keeps helping Snake, keeps fighting the good fight, without ever sacrificing who he is.

Of course, Otacon isn't the hero of *MGS1*. So what would a game with Otacon as the protagonist look like? It would revolve around you destroying your invention, Metal Gear, that you constructed for the purposes of good but is now being manipulated for nefarious purposes. It would still be a stealth game because that would make perfect sense. Otacon is not a character who benefits from an excess of strength or battle experience, so stealth would actually be necessary. The justification for that style of game mechanic would be baked into both narrative and character. Since Otacon is tech savvy, there could be a lot of gameplay that centers around hacking terminals to open doors and to turn off security cameras or lights, providing the player with the possibility of evading conflict entirely. Or Otacon could easily stumble upon weapons caches just like Snake does, and fight to defend himself. Either way, you would still wet yourself, still cry at the death of the woman you loved, but in the end you'd be the hero that killed your own creation to benefit humanity.

And what if our hero, Otacon, met Snake as an NPC? Snake would come off as a huge asshole. He's telling the hero of the story that he has to pull himself together, that he isn't allowed to cry? What a bully. And, funny thing is, something tells me Otacon is more than likely a closer analog for most players than the actual protagonist they control.

So why do we keep inviting kids to play as bullies?[63] And why do we have our rare character exceptions end up becoming emotionally distant and stunted like the people that mock them?

Every Metal Gear game that Otacon is featured in, someone he loves dies. In *MGS1*, it's Sniper Wolf.

---

63 **Anthony:** Because publishers and developers are too scared of taking those kinds of chances, mainly. The fear that something might not be "badass enough" is pretty pervasive in the games industry.

Then, in *MGS2* we meet Emma Emmerich, Otacon's stepsister, a young girl with an awesome bird. The two have a complex past. They used to be incredibly close, but after a series of horrifying things happen to Emma— her father committing suicide and nearly drowning her in the process, then almost getting sexually assaulted— she comes to resent Otacon for not protecting her... just in time to be killed by a weird asshole named Vamp. Then, in *MGS4*, he ends up falling for Naomi of *MGS1* fame and she kills herself—while the same music that plays during Sniper Wolf's death in *MGS1* mournfully plays in the background. The only person we've seen reciprocate affection with Otacon dies by her own hand. Oh, and for an added knife-twist, Naomi was helping Vamp—the guy that killed Emma. So, she betrays him just a few ticks before she takes her own life. Radical. "Why does it always end this way?" Otacon cries after Naomi dies. "Just when I thought I was ready to fall in love." The fact that Naomi's death scene almost exactly mirrors Sniper Wolf's is the greatest evidence of the game's emotional manipulation. You couldn't even think of a different way for her to die? You want to do it *exactly* the same way so we can remember again how fucked Otacon's life is?

And to what end? So he can say this after Snake tells him to pull himself together, "I'm done crying. *I don't have any more tears to shed.*"

On one hand, Otacon's echo of Snake's sentiment is pretty elegant. In *MGS1*, Otacon was a naive, idealistic, starry-eyed guy. After three major deaths in his life, and seeing a shit-ton of war and bloodshed, he too doesn't have any tears to shed. On the other hand, I just spent several hundred words explaining that the main reason I liked Otacon in *MGS1* is because he *isn't* Snake. By *MGS4*, Kojima is just choosing to create yet another Strong Silent Dude Who's Become Emotionally Inaccessible Because of his Dark Past.

We often approach video games with a lot of assumptions about what players want. Players need to be a dude, a man's man, a buff badass who don't take no shit. Sure it'd be nice to make a game with Otacon at the helm, but no one would play it.

But this assumption about what types of protagonists young men want to play as isn't based on hard evidence. In fact, in a study I did with Rosalind Wiseman in 2015 about the gaming habits of boys and girls, we found evidence to the contrary. We surveyed 1,583 students—male and female—about their gaming preferences, and asked them various questions about what sorts of protagonists they like to play as and want to see. The vast majority of students (over 70% for both genders) said they are not more likely to play a game based on the gender of the protagonist, and only 39% of high school-aged boys even cared about playing as a man at all.

Our study focused more on gender itself than the personality of a protagonist, but the evidence points to a relevant conclusion: Boys don't care that much about who they play as. Macho wish fulfillment isn't high on their list of priorities, which means that protagonists like Snake shouldn't be treated as a foregone conclusion.

We don't have many Otacons in games. They're special when they come up, especially in a franchise as big as Metal Gear. But after systematically and unnecessarily killing off everyone Otacon loved most, Kojima sucked that air out of the room, and pumped in thick machismo gas. The kind that makes your throat hurt and your eyes water, but not like you're crying, because buff dudes don't cry.

They seem to have lost all their tears somewhere.

GRAY FOX & LIQUID SNAKE

ANTHONY

If Otacon represents an overabundance of human emotion and empathy in a world where those have no real place, Gray Fox signifies the opposite. He's the most adept fighter in the series (until, in *MGS4*, Kojima basically retconned Raiden into wielding the power of

Neo multiplied by Toshiro Mifune), but he's lost the ability to feel emotions other than pain and anger.

It speaks volumes about the quality of Fox's characterization that it has, despite his death at the end of *MGS1*, managed to survive through the rest of the series. Yes, Gray Fox is a weird cyborg ninja, but he's a cyborg ninja with a purpose. Kojima didn't shove cyborg ninjas into *MGS2* and *MGS4 just* because cyborg ninjas are awesome, but also because Fox both encapsulated many of the series's overarching themes about inhumanity and the use of soldiers as tools, and did so while engendering curiosity and sympathy.

Gray Fox refers to himself as "neither enemy nor friend," and unlike the vast majority of would-be antiheroes who bark similar rubbish (Riddick, Mad Max, Dexter Morgan), he's as morally ambiguous as he claims to be. Fox may help the player navigate minefields and defeat Liquid Snake, but he also really, really, *really* wants to murder Snake. He may be a sympathetic soul because of his brotherly relationship with Naomi, but he still murdered the shit out of her parents.

Gray Fox doesn't cleanly fit into his role. The first time I played through the game, I found him especially villainous just for how much trouble his boss fight gave me. Even though Fox technically helps you out more frequently than he hurts, I still held a lot of anger toward him after he killed me a dozen times. To this day, I can still perform his "clashing of bone and sinew" monologue word-for-word—that's how many times I had to hear it. I so badly wanted to kill Gray Fox for most of my first playthrough, but the moment he committed his last act of (insanely violent) self-sacrifice, I couldn't help but forgive him. Like Psycho Mantis and Sniper Wolf, he's a tortured monster. But *unlike* Mantis and Wolf, Snake cares about him. Even beyond their shared history in *Metal Gear 2: Solid Snake* (which I hadn't played), Gray Fox represents Snake's potential dark side—what Snake could become if he goes too far.

Otacon, Gray Fox, and Snake compose a triad: *This* is what happens if you're too emotional, *this* is what happens if you're too coldhearted, and *this* is what happens if you can combine those traits in perfect proportions. If you've ever watched the original *Star Trek*, you should be familiar with this dynamic: Bones represents empathy and passion, Spock represents cold logic, and Kirk represents the middle ground where passion and logic conflict but ultimately reconcile.

Even though Snake accuses Otacon of being too soft, it is Snake who almost breaks down in tears right before his "love can bloom on a battlefield" monologue. As he looks ruefully into the distance, he says, "In the movies, the hero always saves the girl…" It's an awkward, cheesy precursor to an awkward, cheesy monologue. It's also the only thing keeping Snake from turning into a merciless cyborg killer like Gray Fox.

Until his final moments, Fox never expresses an interest in anything other than being punched in the face or slicing dudes' arms off. He was bred to be the perfect soldier and, apart from the fact that he can't tell friend from foe, that's what he is. It's only in his final moments that Fox acknowledges his mistakes. He reveals that he murdered Naomi's parents, and that he regrets lying to her for so many years. With this weight lifted from his conscience, Fox asks Snake to tell Naomi the truth shortly before getting shot, de-limbed, stabbed, and squashed.

There's a problem, though: Naomi loved Gray Fox like a brother. He raised her after the (to her mind, random) death of her parents.

With this new information about Naomi, Snake has to make a choice: Does he fulfill Gray Fox's last wishes and tell Naomi that her de facto brother is the same man who orphaned her? Naomi *did* poison Snake to get revenge for nearly killing Gray Fox in the first place. Strategically, it's the right thing to do. The "honorable" thing to do. The tough thing to do.

Snake doesn't do it.

"He had one last message he wanted to say to you," Snake says. "He told me to tell you to forget about him and to go on with your own life… He also said he'll always love you. Naomi, your brother just saved you, me, and the whole world. He fought with every ounce of strength in his body."

Gray Fox wanted to repent for his crimes, but he lacked the empathy to understand what revealing this truth would have done to Naomi. Losing her brother in body *and* in spirit would have been too much to bear. Fox repents in the best way he knows how—telling the truth—but Snake, who has never hesitated to tell someone what he thinks ("I'm the pawn they sent here to save your worthless butt," he tells the DARPA chief at the game's opening), has learned that compassion might be more important than brute force.

ASH

I feel conflicted about Snake's choice in this moment. I agree with you that it's an elegant reflection of Snake's arc. His choice to lie to Naomi is an indication that he's actually considering her feelings, which is not something he would've done at the beginning of the game.

But in a way, it seems unfair that Snake should make that choice for her. That information directly concerns Naomi and came from someone with whom she has a deep emotional connection—it belongs to her. Snake, a tourist in this relationship, acting as intermediary for crucial information, feels… wrong. Who is he to decide whether Naomi should hear the truth about her brother? Shouldn't she have had the choice?

I wonder what that moment would've felt like had the player been given a choice of whether or not to tell her about Gray Fox's past. It would've disrupted the crafted story-driven experience that Kojima constructed, but it would've been an interesting opportunity for the player to shape that narrative—to decide what sort of Snake the events of this game have created. Is your Snake the type of Snake that is sick of secrecy and deception, and will trust Naomi with Gray Fox's message despite the pain it will cause her? Or, in his affection for Naomi, will he keep the secret to himself to preserve her positive memories of her brother?

Either way, that moment would say a lot about the man Snake is, and the man he is turning into.

ANTHONY

I see where you're coming from, and it again highlights the weirdness of playing as Snake: You get to determine *some* important parts of his personality, but not others. To me, the Naomi/Fox beat is about giving Snake a clear character arc at all costs. Yes, Kojima could have made that moment a dialogue choice—in fact, I'm now imagining how good a Telltale Games version of *Metal Gear Solid* could be—but choosing to tell Naomi the truth would have meant that Snake probably hadn't learned much. He would have started the game as a blunt asshole and ended as one. It's not perfect, but Snake's relationship with Fox and Naomi does a lot of heavy lifting in terms of developing Snake.

In fact, Fox is so effective in progressing Snake's character arc that he undermines the primary conflict in the game: Solid Snake vs. Liquid Snake.

I love voice actor Cam Clarke's egomaniacal portrayal of Liquid Snake as much as any self-respecting *Metal Gear Solid* fan, but Liquid himself just isn't up to the task as the game's antagonist. Unlike nearly all the underlings Liquid has hired to protect him, the blonder Snake just isn't sympathetic.

Liquid Snake's motivations are, in descending order of importance:

1. *I loved my dad, so I wanna be like him.*
2. *You killed my dad, so I wanna kill you.*
3. *You also got all our dad's good genes. I'm jealous, cuz those genes were fucking sick.*

Liquid doesn't feel like a scary, three-dimensional foe so much as a little twerp who got picked last in dodgeball. His jealousy and rage make him feel more impotent than imposing.

Granted, it doesn't help that he's also a humorless doof, and the game's attempts to make a real character out of Liquid are too clever, too late. Early on in the game, several characters mention how similar Snake and Liquid look. This is meant to make us all curious: Who could he possibly be, and what is his relationship to Snake?

In practice, it's not all that hard to guess. They both go by "Snake" and they're visually identical, so even my ten-year-old brain quickly surmised that they were probably clones. Liquid spends 90% of the game being vague and pseudo-mysterious, time that could have been better spent delivering actual characterization. Liquid suffers from the same storytelling mistake that plagues so much of modern cinema: assuming that if you show a character acting like a dick and then wait until the end to show *why* they're a dick, the audience will find them more interesting and sympathetic than if they'd just known why the dick was a dick to begin with. This is a waste of the audience's time. We stick to our first impression of a character, and if we aren't immediately given sufficient reason to care about why they are the way they are, then no number of late, twisty-turny character backstory reveals will make us care about them in retrospect.[64]

This is why Liquid talks for almost twenty minutes straight when you finally face him. You can feel Kojima rushing to jam in as much characterization as he can because he wasted so much screen time faffing about.

---

64   **Anthony:** For more on this storytelling mistake, read *Screenwriting 101* by Film Crit Hulk!

Much like *Lost* and *Doctor Who* at their worst, Liquid's arc is too obsessed with Mystery and Surprise and Big Reveals, all to the detriment of character and drama.

"Wait a minute," you might be thinking. "Isn't this the kind of deathbed characterization you applauded when it came to Psycho Mantis, Gray Fox, and Sniper Wolf? Why does it work for those characters but not Liquid?"

Quite simply, they don't draw the same amount of narrative attention that Liquid does.

While you don't learn anything sympathetic about Psycho Mantis or Sniper Wolf until their dying breaths, this works perfectly fine because we don't spend much time with these characters in the first place. Not only that, we aren't asked to think about those characters near as frequently as we're asked to think about Liquid. Throughout the game, we are constantly reminded that Liquid is somebody we need to care about—he's a bad dude, he's dangerous, he's your equal, and you've got to stop him. By contrast, Mantis and Wolf just exist—they're around when the plot needs them, and absent when it doesn't. We're free to care as much or as little about them as we like. If Mantis and Wolf were boring or unsympathetic, it wouldn't matter. When Liquid is boring, the plot suffers. He's our end-goal, after all, and we should feel personally invested in taking him out.

Even though he switches allegiances nearly every time he shows up onscreen, Gray Fox is still more immediately interesting and well-rounded than Liquid. The first moment we meet Gray Fox, he cuts off Ocelot's hand and saves ArmsTech president Kenneth Baker. The second time we meet him, he's brutally murdered a dozen security guards and wants to kill us—he clearly *enjoys* killing. The questions he makes us ask—*Who is this man, and what does he want?*—don't have obvious answers. And when we learn those answers, they're all the better for their simplicity: It's Snake's old pal Gray Fox, and he wants to die on the battlefield.

NAOMI & COLONEL CAMPBELL

ASH

Gray Fox is also responsible for the backstory of Naomi, FOXHOUND's resident scientist and doctor. In fact, Naomi's story revolves entirely around men—both the man she intends to revenge, and the man who killed him. She even tells Snake that he was "all she thought about for two years—like some sort of twisted obsession," mirroring Sniper Wolf's own obsession with Snake.

Which blows, because Naomi is otherwise the most interesting female character in the game. She has a complicated and emotionally layered relationship with

Snake, who killed her benefactor and brother, Gray Fox. Naomi concedes that she joined the mission to get close to Snake so that she could kill him after he killed those she needed and loved. Her subterfuge and manipulation—leading you to believe she's an ally, when in fact she intends to murder you—makes her immediately more interesting than her fellow women. It suggests a greater level of depth and independent thought than Nastasha or Mei Ling, two women who are prominently featured in the game, but still manage to be as interesting and useful as wet wads of paper.

Mei Ling is the barely-veiled save point for your game, but since *MGS1* doesn't shy away from breaking the fourth wall, that duty could've been delegated to any other character without the player even batting an eyelash. In a game where you're instructed to plug your controller into the player two port to confuse a *crazy, levitating psychic*, you don't need to narratively justify your saving system. Outside of that, Mei Ling is useless (and also racist?).[65] [66] Nastasha is relevant to the 1%

---

65   **Ash:** She's a US-born character of Chinese heritage who speaks almost exclusively in Chinese proverbs with a heavy accent. It's hard to tell if this is some weird hiccup of localization or just straight up racism. It's a toss up with *MGS1*.

66   **Anthony:** Also, when they brought the character back for *MGS4*, they ditched the accent. A decade's worth of hindsight probably made them realize exactly what you're saying.

of players who enjoy gun tutorials, and contributes nothing to the game outside of that.

Naomi, on the other hand, has an arc! After hating Snake violently for two years, meeting and working with him in person muddles her anger and confuses her fury. Throughout the game, Naomi chooses to relinquish her desire for revenge and instead "chooses life." Naomi then alters FOXDIE, a virus the Pentagon spreads through its carrier, Snake, to cover up the events of the mission. It isn't clear exactly what Naomi changes in the virus, but by doing so, she's the only female character who affects the plot in a meaningful way. Which is why it's extra unfortunate that Naomi's story is grounded in the lives of men.

But at least she has plenty more going on than Colonel Campbell, the leader of your covert mission who carries roughly 70% of the dialogue and does nothing of interest for about 90% of the game.

If you care enough to keep track of the wild twists and turns of *Metal Gear Solid*'s story, you'll notice that Snake says something along the lines of, "Colonel, are you hiding something from me?" seven times throughout the course of the game.[67] Every time, Campbell is hiding something, and every time, the truth comes out. Snake begrudgingly swallows each small betrayal and Campbell

---

67   **Anthony:** Not an exaggeration. We counted.

pleads for Snake to do what the narrative is requiring of him at that moment. Which Snake does. Until Campbell betrays him again. Then the scenario rinses and repeats, each betrayal as predictable as the last.

Campbell's actions have some justification—he's much more grounded, and his decisions are more sympathetic than, say, Vulcan Raven, who just likes to kill people and talk about birds a lot.[68] Campbell is being lorded over by mysterious higher-ups trying to mask a conspiracy, and you eventually discover that Meryl is his daughter and they were using her as leverage to keep him in line. However, apart from breaking the fourth wall every once in a while to give you a pointer, hiding information is just about all Campbell does. You don't have any moments with the Colonel about his backstory, no long lamentations about his past or his fight with his own genetics. He exists to keep Snake in the dark.

Snake ends up finding out all the pertinent plot information on his own, and Campbell only ends up confirming it. As far as the player is concerned, Campbell is essentially useless. Until the end of the game, the most direct impact he has on the narrative is that twenty some odd years ago, he got Meryl's mom pregnant.

---

68   **Raven:** "The raven on my head... It thirsts for his blood!"

Instead, the Colonel is a tonal device. So instead of giving the player narrative information, he exists to give you the sense that the conspiracy in this plot goes *deep*. His betrayal makes the world seem a bit darker, creating a sense that the player is truly on their own—that betrayal could come from anywhere. But his betrayal loses its punch after the first or second time. It just keeps happening, again and again. Almost as if Kojima is prodding you with his elbow, wiggling his eyebrows and going, "Eh? Eh? The plot *thickens*, eh?" Campbell is almost a stand-in for the developer. He teaches you how to play the game and then constantly teases you with secrets to keep you engaged in the story.

And yet, long after we've all written him off, even Campbell gets his moment to play hero. At the end of the game, Campbell calls off a firebombing strike on Shadow Moses ordered by the Secretary of Defense, effectively saving Snake, Otacon, and Meryl's lives.[69] After several hours of deception, double crossing, and attempts on your life, Campbell's decision to do a nice thing cancels out his constant and unsurprising pseudo-betrayals.

---

69   **Ash:** Or, just Snake and Otacon's lives if Meryl died earlier. Sorry Meryl.

ANTHONY

Kojima actually uses video game conventions to make this moment of characterization work as well as it does. After you've shirtlessly punched Liquid off Metal Gear REX, you're informed that a countdown has begun. Secretary of Defense Jim Houseman has ordered a bunch of jets to obliterate Shadow Moses and bury all evidence of the US's involvement in all the Metal Gear project, genome soldiers, and shirtless punching.

Because this is a cheesy video game, and because *all* cheesy video games end with us having to escape a base before it blows up (*Super Metroid*, *Fallout*, *The Legend of Zelda: Ocarina of Time*, etc.), we are set up to wholeheartedly believe that Shadow Moses will be destroyed the second we escape. Not to mention that Otacon has locked himself inside the base so he can help you escape—he's reaching the end of a pretty clear Coward Becomes Self-Sacrificial Hero character arc, and the Secretary of Defense's bombers will likely be the explosive exclamation point to his character growth. Our subconscious understanding of video game cliché and character arcs make us pretty damned sure that once Meryl drives our jeep screaming out of the Shadow Moses tunnels, the Fox archipelago is gonna erupt in flame behind us.

But then… it doesn't. Campbell successfully calls off the fighter attack.

As a kid, I was fully prepared for an orgasmically large explosion to cap off my time with *Metal Gear Solid*. Thanks to Campbell's actions, however, the game ends on a much quieter note.

This moment works because it's based in *character*. Kojima could have come up with dozens of reasons for the base to not explode, but he wisely decided to use the scene to develop Campbell's character arc. Campbell starts the game as a guy who follows orders even when it means lying to his best friend. He ends the game as a dude who is basically willing to fistfight the goddamn Secretary of Defense. It's a bait-and-switch: You think you're going to get a generic, video gamey ending, only for Campbell to intervene and help end the game on a quieter, more somber note. No explosions. Just a supervillain dying of the sniffles (blah blah blah FOXDIE was programmed to kill him blah blah), and a couple of cute caribou hanging out on a frozen lake.[70]

ASH

So is it sort of manipulative of Kojima to change our whole opinion of Campbell in one nice action? Probably. But the fact that Anthony and I are writing a

---

70 **Anthony:** Kojima's team presumably concepted, 3D modeled, and animated those two caribou just for the sake of symbolism. Which is, perhaps, not that surprising given Kojima's creation and immediate abandonment of the snow footprint mechanic.

book about this game over fifteen years after we played it means that this cast of characters—the well-crafted weirdos and the hamfisted Brits alike—must've worked on some level.

That's the funny thing about Kojima. He never follows the rules, but he always seems to get away with it.

MERYL?

My name is Meryl. And I've always wanted to be a soldier.

...That's it. I can't express another desire I've ever had that wasn't wanting to be a soldier.

Someone asked me if I wanted a bagel once and I was like, "Will this help me be a soldier?" and they were like, "Uh, I mean, it's food so... I guess?"

It was only then that I ate the bagel.

Only then did I eat the bagel.

But then I met Snake.

Maybe it was the way he stared at my butt and then called me a rookie. Maybe it was the way he punched me unconscious when I was being controlled by an evil psychic. Whatever it was, I knew. After roughly 40 minutes... I knew.

I didn't want to be a soldier anymore. I was in love. Snake was all I needed.

If someone offered me a bagel now, I'd be like, "Does Snake like it when I eat bagels?" and if they said no, I wouldn't eat it, and if they said yes, I would eat it.

I would eat that bagel. For him.
Forever.

ASH

For a few years in my adolescence, I was convinced that female characters were inherently less cool than male characters. If given the opportunity in a fighting game, I thought it made me cooler and less "typically girly" to choose to play as a dude. I shunned games marketed toward girls, and scoffed openly at the Spice Girls' anthems of "girl power."

I was, essentially, the littlest misogynist.[71]

This phase happened to coincide with the height of *MGS1*'s popularity in our household. I felt cool for playing something so gritty and took pride in every successfully evaded guard because it meant I was *good* at the game. Liking the game was a badge of honor— proof that I was not a "normal girl."

With Snake's guidance, *MGS1* reinforced all of the shitty things I felt about myself and my gender. Girls aren't as strong as boys. It's cooler to not show your feelings. The Snakes of the world would like and respect me if I was more like them.

---

71   **Anthony:** A children's book by /r/theredpill I would not read.

Adult Ashly wishes she could go back and tell young Ashly that *Metal Gear Solid* doesn't offer an accurate depiction of my gender. That just because pop culture tells me that my gender is weak and helpless, it doesn't mean that we are. That the script for *MGS1* was written by a middle-aged dude who *really* likes boobs and that I shouldn't let it affect my view of myself.

Which brings us to Meryl. Dear sweet boring Meryl.

Meryl is the prize to be won. The damsel in need of rescuing. The cardboard cutout woman who exists to give Snake motivation and make his emotional arc meaningful. In true *Metal Gear Solid* fashion, there's a hefty amount of cognitive dissonance that goes along with this reality. Meryl's a soldier! She's smart enough to disguise herself in enemy clothing. She can sneak around highly guarded areas undetected. She helps you find important plot items.

And she's completely, offensively boring.[72]

When I was a kid, I found it hilarious that 80% of Meryl's lines included the phrase "I wanted to be a soldier." Even as an eight-year-old, I understood how absurd it was that Meryl's one piece of definitive characterization was repeated ad infinitum—as if having her say her one motivation over and over could make her a complex character.

---

72 **Anthony:** At the time, I thought she was cool because she was a redhead. Then I figured out I was just into redheads.

And truly, that's only a piece of Meryl's story we're given. During the course of the game, she apparently learns that being a soldier is "ugly" and terrible. Never mind that while that may actually be true, the game makes war seem rad—you take down an enormous *dinosaur-robot* with a *missile launcher*, for chrissake.[73] Apart from that, we know that Meryl is naive, eager to prove herself, she likes Snake and… that's it? We get the general gist that she's "good," but no real sense of what that means.

In the first conversation with Otacon, we learn that he's idealistic, naive, cowardly, innovative, intelligent, nerdy, socially awkward, and emotional. We learn his backstory, his moral conflict, his interests. We understand why he's motivated to help the player. His arc is influenced by Snake, but is still predominantly about him learning to take a stand and break the cycle of nuclear warfare embedded in his family history. We can watch Otacon transform from a man of fearful compliance to a brave, determined ally.

Meryl's arc is from someone who doesn't like Snake to someone who really likes Snake.

Thus, her romance with Snake becomes the centerpiece of her story. What makes it even worse is that Snake spends the game oscillating between treating

---

73 **Anthony:** Fun fact: This is how WWII ended.

her like incompetent garbage and giving her creepy compliments. The first time he meets her, he calls her a rookie five times. In their next conversation, Snake gives her a misplaced, saccharine compliment about her "beautiful, compassionate eyes." Then, in a heartfelt callback to their first date, he calls her a rookie again, and follows it up with a demand that she hide, lest she be hurt. The conversation ends with Snake telling her to "stay the hell out of [his] way," then they have a good guffaw (for some reason?), and Meryl concedes to flee for her safety and actually utters the phrase, "I'll be a good girl." Does that give anyone else the willies? Are you an eight-year-old addressing your dad? If you saw two adult humans having this interaction in real life, would you be anything other than grossed the fuck out?

But wait. It gets grosser.

When Snake first meets Meryl, she's dressed as an enemy combatant. There's a shot of her bolting for an elevator because she distrusts Snake and wants to get the hell out of dodge. As she runs away, there is an *extreme, slow-mo close-up on her ass.*

No exaggeration—time actually slows down so that Snake and the player can take a good, long look at Meryl's sweet, blocky butt. But don't worry, it's not like it's in there *just* so dudes can gawk at her hind quarters. It's actually a game mechanic!

That's right. In a cinematic stealth game about the horrors of nuclear warfare, you are required to stare at a woman's ass to advance the plot.

ANTHONY

This scene is objectifying. It's sexist. It undermines the game's attempts to characterize Meryl as a smart, tough, self-possessed woman.

It's also, infuriatingly, one of the only interesting gameplay twists in the series. Where many of the game's one-off challenges ask the player to disregard all of the stealth mechanics upon which the game is based, the Butt Mission encourages the player to gain a deeper understanding of enemy patrols, vision cones, and proximity.

The "correct" way to solve Butt Mission requires the player to get close to an enemy while they're moving (so the player can look at Dat Butt), understand when the enemy will turn around (so the player knows when Snake might be spotted staring at Dat Butt), and use the otherwise-useless first-person view mode to more closely inspect their target('s butt). You've by now become used to treating all enemies like identical cannon fodder, but Butt Mission asks you to slow down, examine each soldier carefully, and find the one with a *slightly* more bootylicious walk than the others, and make sure *not* to kill her.[74]

Here, for once, is a problem that can't be solved by simply shooting the enemy from a distance with a silenced pistol, or grabbing them by the neck and killing them in two seconds. The Butt Mission is more suspenseful and nuanced than the more bombastic, less sexist moments that surround it.

There is no single moment in all of *Metal Gear Solid* that so perfectly encapsulates the game's highs and lows with such clarity. It is so sexist and embarrassing that it is nearly hilarious… but it is also one of the game's best-designed moments. It is the most mature, least mature scene in the game.

Metal Gear Solid IS the butt mission.

ASH

Meryl, unaware that her ass has been a topic of *much* conversation (Otacon and Snake have a moment where they admire Meryl's butt together) asks Snake how he recognized her.

> Snake: I never forget a lady.

---

74 **Anthony:** The "incorrect" solution: Just run into the vision cone of every guard and die until one of them eventually turns out to be Meryl.

Meryl: So there's something you like about me, huh?

Snake: Yeah. You've got a great butt.

Meryl (not at all bothered): Oh, I see. First it's my eyes, now it's my butt. What's next?

Snake: On the battlefield, you never think about what's next.

Putting aside for a moment that the exchange shifts from butts to stoic ruminations of life on the battlefield with no self-awareness about how weird and unintentionally funny that is, this scene pretty neat summarizes both the schizophrenic nature of *MGS1* and how the game depicts Snake's relationships with women. Which is to say, he acts like a creep and a dick.

The problem is less that Snake is a condescending ass to Meryl than it is that she has *no* problem with being treated that way. In fact, Meryl's super into it. She's on the Snake-town express and she's riding it until it goes off the rails. The most she does to defy him is to periodically insist that she's capable and won't slow him down while proceeding to disprove those claims at every opportunity. She gets brainwashed, then shot, then kidnapped, until each of Snake's demeaning comments about her is validated. As she lays in the snow bleeding after being shot multiple times by a high-powered sniper rifle, Meryl manages to choke out the words, "I guess I am a rookie after all."

Sweeeeeeet. Now Meryl is *finally* on board with how dumb and useless she is. All it took was getting shot a bunch of times.

Just in time to be kidnapped and incapacitated.

Snake also gets kidnapped, but he still retains his agency. The player is treated to a mini-game in which Snake has to endure a tremendous amount of pain so that Liquid's nasty posse will let Meryl live. A manlier scenario has never been conceived. Snake would need to be horking down T-bone steaks to up the machismo level of that challenge. Provided you don't cave into the torture, Meryl will be waiting for you after your almost-but-not-quite-final confrontation with Liquid. As she hazily returns to consciousness, she tells you:

> I didn't give into the torture… *and things even worse than that…* During all the *pain and shame* there was one thing I was sure of… a single hope that I held onto… And that hope kept me alive… Snake, I wanted to see you again…

Here, Meryl reveals two pieces of information: (a) that a man she met mere hours ago is her number one reason for living, and (b) that she was raped. (Her delivery of this line, with quivering voice and a clear sense of personal violation, sell this interpretation.) As Adult Burches,

Anthony and I were shocked by (b), as that particular piece of dialogue flew right over our heads as kids. But, playing it as an adult, the message came through as loud and clear as if she'd said the actual word. And why did they decide to just throw that in there as if it were as casual as her telling us her favorite color?

1. To make the game seem more real and gritty because that's important in a game where mechs roar like dinosaurs.
2. To make the player want to protect her even more.
3. Because… so she could like… be more… sad? What?

ANTHONY

My fear is this moment didn't even get *that* much thought—female characters get sexually abused because That's Just What You Do. Lazy writers use sexual abuse to raise stakes or make the bad guys seem bad. Christ, *Metal Gear Solid V: Ground Zeroes* ends with a teenage girl exploding thanks to a bomb forcibly inserted into her vagina.[75]

ASH

If the player endures Revolver Ocelot's torture, Meryl lives, and you're rewarded with a throwaway reference to

---

75   **Ash:** THANKS, KOJIMA.

her sexual assault, some awkwardly lovey-dovey dialogue, and the promise of a new happy life between Meryl and Snake. She also gives you a bandana that grants you unlimited ammo for a subsequent playthrough, to ignore the "stealth" part of "tactical stealth espionage" and go full Rambo. Conversely, if you end the game with Otacon (i.e. if Meryl dies), he gives you his sneaking suit.

It's always cool when games incentivize multiple playthroughs through alternate endings—it feels more meaningful to have different actions produce different gameplay possibilities. But in this case, it also means that you're ultimately saving Meryl or letting her die for an item. Which is a whole new level of objectification. She doesn't even get to be the object herself, she's a means to an actual object. She's the silver key to unlock the treasure chest.

However, if you cave into the torture and Meryl dies, then things shift a bit emotionally for Snake. He cradles her body[76] and tells her he's sorry, that he isn't the hero she thought he was, that he's a failure, that he lost. Otacon arrives and, in much the same way that Snake instructed him to do before, tells Snake to focus on the mission. He references his loss of Sniper Wolf, and says that their love didn't die with her, that he shouldn't give up, blah blah. Eventually, Snake is convinced to save himself, and tells Meryl that he hopes she's watching so he can finally prove himself to her.

76　**Ash:** Which Liquid decided to just, you know, bring along.

This is a bit of a switcheroo on the typical male-power-fantasy formula we've seen reinforced thus far. In this iteration of the narrative, Snake *isn't* strong enough. He *doesn't* save the girl. He's forced to confront his own insufficiencies. For the first time in the game, he shows true vulnerability and regret.[77]

However, after this point, the game proceeds in much the same way that it does if Meryl lives. Snake and Otacon both opt to live life to the fullest, Naomi delivers a long monologue about how your genes don't decide your fate, and everyone—even Campbell—has a generally okay time.

Except for Meryl, who is dead.

Ultimately, Meryl's death is only significant for a few moments of connective dialogue—an obligatory period of mourning that Snake almost immediately snaps out of so he can assume his role as Ultimate Alpha Man. So, in the end, Meryl essentially amounts to nothing more than an accessory to Snake's story. She matters as much as she can motivate him to act, or provide a brief emotional consequence when he doesn't.

For a young boy playing the game, I can imagine that Meryl's dutiful, unconditional affection—whether she dies or not—feels awesome. If you're a self-conscious

---

77   **Anthony:** It's also probably worth noting that this is the non-canonical ending. Kojima clearly didn't want the more vulnerable version of Snake to move forward through the rest of the series.

adolescent boy who wants desperately to interact with girls, Meryl is a dream woman. She's cute, you get to protect her, and she falls in love with you in about three hours. What young boy wouldn't want that?[78]

After my phase of hating all things girly, I made up for lost time by obsessing over the anime *Sailor Moon* to an unreasonable degree. I swooned over Darien because he liked Sailor Moon no matter how annoying or weird she was, he was cute, and every once in while, she got to save him. As a former shy girl who none of the boys liked, I definitely get the appeal of that fantasy.

But I kept playing *Metal Gear Solid* too. I saw Meryl. And when I dabbled in misogyny, she was a great role model. In a rare moment of characterization, she tells Snake that she never wore makeup, and despised women who chose to be feminine. Eight-year-old Ashly strongly related to that. But, it's not like Meryl ever takes the time to say, "However you choose to express gender is absolutely fine and no one can judge you for it," so the conversation ends there. So little-Ashly thought, "Yeah! Fuck feminine women!"

Meryl does everything she does for the recognition of men, either Snake or her absent father, which I also related to. A huge part of my adolescent life was wanting to be accepted by my brother and his friends—people who seemed to be the height of all that was rad and

---

78   **Anthony:** I wanted that.

awesome.[79] Girly things were decidedly not cool to boys at that age, so I downplayed my feminine side.

And, lest we forget, I thought Snake was the dreamiest of dreams, so the fact that Meryl managed to bag him in the end only further stoked the fires of my accidental misogyny.

And that misogyny wasn't easy to extinguish. It took me a little while to grow out of the idea that being "feminine" isn't bad, and that trying to be "masculine" doesn't automatically make you cooler. I had to learn that expressing gender by putting on makeup or wearing skirts isn't a cardinal sin, because while it sucks that women are often expected to adhere to typical standards of feminine beauty, some women just enjoy wearing mascara. I had to accept that I was one of those women. I had to learn that I liked being feminine.

I had to learn that I, as a woman, could be just as awesome as a man, no matter how I do or don't express my femininity.

I was not born with the knowledge that my gender is as capable, smart, cunning, funny, stupid, rude, inconsiderate, insightful, and innovative as men are. I had to learn that. And that's because most of the media I've consumed has espoused crappy ideas about my gender, creating "blank slate" female characters defined by their

---

79   **Anthony:** Correct.

relationships with men and used as motivation for those men to get revenge/complete the mission/come out of retirement/save the world.[80] When that's the only type of woman you see when you're a little girl, it's easy to perpetuate an already well-developed lack of self-worth.

Because there's so much that's ridiculous about *Metal Gear Solid* apart from its representation of women, it's easy to ignore the problems with its female characters and dismiss Kojima as wacky and lovable. But the problem doesn't end with Kojima. It's everywhere. It's still happening constantly. Women are damseled. They're sexualized. They're peripheralized. Meanwhile, in real life, women are 50% of the population. It doesn't make any sense that our popular media features complex men as protagonists, but simplistic, helpless, sexualized women as secondary characters.

And it's not a coincidence that women are subjected to horrific crimes like human trafficking, genital mutilation, and spousal abuse, at epidemic levels. We live in a culture that frequently characterizes women as less-than. We diminish their pain, we use it as a motivator for male protagonists, or even worse, sometimes we even imply that they *deserve* it. Let me be clear: I'm not saying that games and other media *cause* this behavior, but they're doing very little to help dissuade the perspective.

---

80   **Ash:** See: 90% of action films made in the last EVER.

They perpetuate the hostile conditions that allow true violence and abuse of women to persist.

Is this an intentional move by game developers? Do they *want* to denigrate women? I don't think so. Call me an optimist, but I find it unlikely that there's some grand misogynist conspiracy at play in the games industry. These narratives are just so thoroughly baked into our cultural subconscious that they're not even called into question. Which makes it easy to replicate them without thinking, and even easier to consume them without thinking.

ANTHONY

Yup. We did basically the same thing in *Borderlands 2*. We took a female character, gave her a godlike amount of power, and then damseled her in the third act because we couldn't think of a better way to get her offstage.

It's an easy mistake to make. More than that, the vast majority of your audience won't find it at all noteworthy: We've all become so used to women getting shat on that it doesn't really raise much of an eyebrow.

ASH

Which is a great point. I don't now hate Anthony and everyone at Gearbox for doing that. This is an unfortunate side effect of creating *anything*, and it happens to even the most outspoken progressives. For example, I love

Firefly—does it mean I'm stoked that the threat of rape is periodically used to up dramatic stakes?[81] No. And I love the shit out of Joss Whedon. He's doing a lot of good by creating interesting, strong and compelling female characters. That doesn't mean he's infallible.

It's the same with *Metal Gear Solid*. It's *incredibly* problematic, and the series hasn't changed since the first game. Meryl might be the commander of a rat patrol squad in *MGS4*, but she constantly has to be saved by her new beau Johnny, who makes a joke of grabbing women's asses as they pass by to *no consequence*.

As the popularity of games only continues to grow, kids will learn what it means to be brave, smart, silly, responsible and empathetic through the games they play. But most importantly, children—boys *and* girls *and* those that don't identify with either term[82]—will absorb lots of gender cues from games: how women and men should act in the world, what is expected of their gender, what sorts of things they can achieve and be.

Let's make sure we're giving them the right messages.

---

81   **Anthony:** Or that the entire series takes place in a China-inspired future universe and there are no Asian cast members.

82   **Ash:** I know we speak in the gender binary a lot in this book— it's something I'm trying to be conscious of when I do advocacy work. How do I talk about sexism and women's rights without excluding other marginalized groups? Is it more effective to focus on one point at a time, or is inclusiveness most important? I'm still trying to figure it out!

INFLUENCE?

ASH

When I was just a wee-Ashly—

ANTHONY

Let's be clear. You are *still* a wee-Ashly.

ASH

WHEN I WAS A SLIGHTLY MORE WEE-ASHLY, I wanted to be a singer. My life was a series of choirs, vying for solos at the Christmas concert, and a less-than-secret desire to be a real life Ariel from *The Little Mermaid* (this was before I learned to resent all things feminine in my adolescent years).

So when I decided to audition for my middle school musical, *The Music Man*, I had my sights set on Marian Paroo because I was insecure, starved for attention, and I wanted to sing "Till There Was You." But I couldn't just sing and go home—I had to perform a scene. And because my teacher wanted to be the evil drama teacher antagonist in a made-for-TV Disney movie, she forced us to do partner reads in front of the other *forty* kids who were also auditioning.

Suffice it to say, I was fucking terrified. I shook as I descended the choir risers to act for the first time in front of a bunch of eighth graders I didn't know. When it came my turn to speak, I was trembling so bad that I doubt anyone could even make out what I was saying. But it didn't matter to me. Something clicked. Even though I was petrified, I really enjoyed myself. I liked trying to inflect in an organic way. I liked the physicality, the energy of acting off of a fellow actor, the challenge of placing myself into someone else's context. Pretending I was a sexually repressed, foppish woman in the 50s was a blast.

The people in that room didn't realize it, but they watched my life's trajectory change in front of them. I remember walking to the bus after school and deciding that I was going to be an actor. It's a memory that's seared in my brain—I can see exactly when the minecart switched tracks.

After that moment, I consumed every piece of media differently. When I watched films, I honed in entirely on performance. I started collecting favorite actors, and I followed their careers religiously.[83] I was mesmerized by their tics and flourishes, how they could be intimidating, how they softened, how they showed fear, anger, surprise, and joy. But it didn't take me long to notice that the one thing I obsessed over with every performance was their vocal work. Did I believe their inflection in that moment? Could I feel the pain they were holding in their chest when they spoke? Could that line have been funnier if they went up *here* instead of *there*?

Then one day, it hit me: David Hayter in *Metal Gear Solid*.

Like many kids, I consumed an alarming number of cartoons and video games. Somewhere in my half-developed child brain, I knew intellectually that the babies in *Rugrats* were drawn and animated by someone, so some part of me must have known that Chuckie didn't come prepackaged with a voice as soon as he was committed to paper. But internalizing that idea—that it was someone's job to pretend she was a three-year-old boy—was something that didn't connect until that summer afternoon when Anthony and I popped in the *MGS1* demo disc.

---

83 **Ash:** Gary Oldman and Johnny Depp were the big ones for a while. I've lost count of how many times I've watched *The Professional* and *Fear and Loathing in Las Vegas*.

I remember the moment when I saw Snake's polygonal face for the first time, and written beneath it:

Solid Snake
(David Hayter)

I was confused. I thought, "Who is David Hayter? Is Solid Snake his code name and David Hayter his actual name? Why is it in parentheses?"[84]

It took me until the DARPA chief's introduction to realize that this wasn't just some weird narrative contextualization I didn't understand. Those names in the parentheses were the actors! This was like a movie! Kojima wanted you to know who was voicing his characters! It was then that I understood that this was an actual job, that there were people in the world who made a living off of voicing animated characters. It was a life-changing discovery.

That interest, that fixation on vocal performance had a thread, and it connected all the way back to *MGS1*. I didn't realize that I wanted to act when I was playing the game, but I remember being totally enrapt by vocal nuance even back then. I was enamored with the gruffness of David Hayter's voice, how his growl made a stationary image with a furrowed brow come to life, how it told me so much about who Snake was. I loved the raspy, close-to-cracking quality of Debi Mae

---

84   **Ash:** Which is funny given that Snake's actual name is David.

West's voice, and how its timbre made all of Meryl's pained shouts a lot more visceral. George Byrd's[85] Gray Fox was to my childhood like Brad Dourif's Doc Cochran on *Deadwood* is to my adulthood. That shaky, desperate, on the cusp of just *disintegrating*, frenetic energy was so tangible and affecting. It made me scared, and uncomfortable, but I still empathized with him so deeply because of the pain in his performance. And Jennifer Hale's Naomi was understated, conveying cold calculation, sorrow, and revelation through subtle, nuanced choices—which is all the cooler to me now that Hale has become a role model to me.

Of course, there are many people who absolutely *hate* the voice acting in *MGS1*. I've spoken to friends who find the performances over the top and hokey, that Solid Snake is cartoonish and overplayed, and don't even get them started on Liquid Snake.

But there is, to me, a certain earnestness to the performances that so perfectly fits the insane, schizophrenic ride Kojima constructed. The Metal Gear series is not about subtlety, and by raising vocal performance to a heightened level, the acting better serves the soap opera tone and story than more subdued choices would have. In a game where you combat psychopathic psychics and

---

85   **Anthony:** A pseudonym for Greg Eagles. *MGS1* was a non-union production, so almost everyone other than David Hayter had to use fake names. Whoops.

single-handedly shoot an enormous rocket launcher at the helicopter your clone brother is riding in, big performances feel right at home.

In fact, the acting in *MGS1* serves as something of a gaming time capsule. In much the same way that performances in films of the 40s have a distinct, Humphrey Bogart-esque cadence to them—going UP on WORDS so folks know you're SERIOUS—the performances in *MGS1* harken back to a time when games weren't so focused on realism. Spending hours laboring over the intricate details of a tank's hatch for a *Call of Duty* game didn't make sense for games in the 90s because there's only so much you can do with polygons. Everything was unreal, which often made everything feel heightened and magical.

I love the direction modern day voice acting has taken since *MGS1*.

The performances in *The Walking Dead: The Game* brought me to tears, the voice acting in *The Last of Us* is fabulous, and The Mass Effect series (featuring an impeccable performance by Jennifer Hale as the female version of Commander Shepard) showcases some of the most moving, affecting performances I've ever experienced in a game.

But I'll always hold a special place in my heart for the performances in *Metal Gear Solid*. Not just because of game's fun and affecting performances, but also because when something changes the course of your life, it's hard not to remember it with a special dose of fondness.

•

ANTHONY

When I first played *Metal Gear Solid*, I wanted to be either a writer or an actor. Today, I am a writer *and* an actor, sort of.[86]

I'd like to say that my childhood love for *Metal Gear Solid* made my present-day job of writing *Borderlands 2* way easier. I'd love to pull out examples of moments where I borrowed bits of characterization or plot structure from some encyclopedia-thick Kojima Bible I'd penned myself. Maybe it'd be leatherbound. Maybe I'd caress the cover of the old tome (I'd always refer to it as a "tome") and nod solemnly before opening it up and drinking in its majesty.

Can't say any of that, though.

In all honesty, I didn't think much about *Metal Gear Solid* after becoming a game dev. I thought a lot about *BioShock*, *Portal*, and the show *Firefly*, but I don't think I ever consciously used a moment from *Metal Gear Solid* to help me with my writing.

---

86   **Anthony:** In our web series, "Hey Ash, Whatcha Playin'?", my "acting" is limited to incredulously exclaiming different variations of the phrase, "What are you talking about?"

Part of this is because my tastes have moved on. There's another reason, though, which didn't occur to me until now:

Metal Gear Solid is not cynical.

It's many things—weird, hilarious, epic, sexist, tonally sporadic—but it is certainly not cynical, sarcastic, or angry. Its characters speak from the heart. They say what they feel, even if that means a twenty-minute monologue on nuclear weapons.

I used to work that way. In elementary school, I was all smiles and high-fives. In kindergarten, I was happy, friendly, and most horrifying of all, *popular*.[87] [88]

Luckily, eight consecutive years in a socially insulated Gifted Program solved all those problems. I was isolated from the normal kids, implicitly told I was better than everyone else. This made me an egocentric douche, which made the normal kids resent me, which made me resent myself *and* them all at the same time. I disliked myself as much as they did—I considered myself a fraud and an asshole. Since junior high, I've operated on a strict diet of cynicism and self-deprecation.

---

87   **Ash:** I also remember that in kindergarten you once got in an hour-long argument with another kid about whether or not Bowser's true name was King Koopa. We had different metrics for what was popular back then.

88   **Anthony:** That was junior high and I still shudder thinking about that every few weeks so thanks for bringing it up super psyched nice one nice nice nice.

Metal Gear Solid, which I fell in love with long before junior high, displayed a fearlessness I can no longer relate to. Whenever I write, I second-guess myself. Is this too indulgent? Is this joke too off-color? Is this character being too cheesy? Why am I even doing this? What happens when everyone finds out I'm not actually good and just got lucky a couple of times?

I don't think Kojima asks himself these questions. A self-deprecator wouldn't take the risks he does. His unapologetic fearlessness is what made the Metal Gear Solid games what they are, for better and worse. Conversely, my cynicism and frustratingly masculine fear of earnestness probably shaped more of my work on *Borderlands 2* than I'd care to admit.

Handsome Jack, the villain of *Borderlands 2*, laughs a lot. He cracks jokes and uses sarcasm as a weapon. The player's friends, the Vault Hunters from the original *Borderlands*, are written with a similar level of snarky detachment. Lilith is arrogant and sarcastic. Mordecai is a cynical drunk. Brick is a bloodthirsty joker who thinks it's funny when you kill his own men. Only Roland, the soldier and leader of the good guys, is a decent human being. He's a nice guy, and he cares about people.

We killed him off, of course.

And not in a selfless or heroic way, either: We had Jack shoot him in the back and then crack a joke about it. In the first draft of Roland's death scene, we even thought it'd be funny if Jack grabbed Roland's corpse and used it like a ventriloquist dummy.

"Aww, poor Roland. Do you think the Vault Hunter has a chance of stopping me?"

(Jack grabs Roland's head and shakes it back and forth.)

"Looks like Roland thinks you suck just as much as I do. Ha!"

Later, we thought it would be funny to twist the knife even harder and put the player into a locked room filled with gun turrets, all trained at the player's face. Suddenly, Jack would contact you over the radio and narrate your death in a knowingly cheesy voice.

"With a dozen guns pointed at them and no means of escape, things looked grim for the Vault Hunter," Jack would say. "But wait—what's that? In the sky!"

Spotlights burst to life, illuminating the ceiling. A trap door slowly opens.

"It's your old pal Roland, come to save you at last!"

Suddenly, Roland's dead body falls gracelessly out of the trapdoor and *THUMPS* awkwardly onto the ground like a sack of potatoes.

"Oh, right. I guess not. I forgot he was *fucking dead*. Later, loser!"

I can't even begin to imagine a Metal Gear villain doing something as mean-spirited as that, just as I can't imagine writing anything as sincere as Sniper Wolf's death monologue. I wrote lots of fun and optimistic stories as a kid,[89] but sometime after playing *MGS1* I turned into the sort of person who would use a hero's corpse for two separate bits of physical comedy.

Even though I don't agree with the narrative philosophies behind the Metal Gear Solid games, they still hold a romantic appeal to me. They show the great and terrible power of an unchained auteur who believes that free will is bullshit and that all people are inherently good. Kojima's narrative and personal philosophies are probably the opposite of my own.

What's interesting about Kojima is that despite his unwavering confidence in himself, he puts himself in an incredibly vulnerable position. Speaking to vg247 about *Metal Gear Solid V: Ground Zeroes,* he said, "I'm going to be treading a lot of taboos and a lot of mature themes that are quite risky… even if I did release the game, maybe it wouldn't sell… but as a creator I want to take that risk. As a producer it's my job to try and sell the game, but I'm approaching this project from the point of view of a creator. I'm prioritizing creativity over sales."

On one hand, I look at that quote and think of how borderline-arrogant it is. *I'm happy calling myself the creator of a game whose staff consists of hundreds of people!*

---

89   **Anthony:** My magnum opus: "Nick Poodoo: Action Scientist," a Half-Life fanfiction.

On the other hand, there's a distinct vulnerability there. He knows that his work might not connect with people, and he's willing to take sole blame if it doesn't.

That's the big difference between sincerity and cynicism. Cynicism keeps everyone at arm's length. If you hide behind sarcasm and wry jokes and winking insincerity, you can't ever really be hurt. Yeah, people said some mean stuff about *Borderlands 2*, but I can always wave my hand and say, "eh—it's a comedy game about shooting bandits in the face with a lightning shotgun." There are a few scattered moments of genuine emotion in *BL2*'s story, but they're buried under snark and cynicism. If I think about it, I've never had a legitimate discussion with anyone about what *BL2* is trying to say—about what it means.

Kojima, meanwhile, made a game about a cyborg ninja fighting a metal Godzilla and he still managed to spend pages and pages on nuclear deterrence, genetic fate, and the cost of war. As a writer, I can sit back in my chair and attack Kojima's writing. It's inelegant and self-indulgent, I can say, to have your characters spout monologues about life for pages at a time. I can say it ruins the pacing, or jars with the game's overall tone, or that it isn't making the experience more fun. Even Jeremy Blaustein, the localization writer for *MGS1*, said of the game: "I also personally think *MGS* should have had a lot less text, A LOT. We really didn't need all the talking about the history of the Cold War and I don't think that many people would disagree with that."

But in the end, Kojima still has the courage to say something. He may say it loudly and he may say it inarticulately, but he says it. More than that, he says it earnestly.

A part of me wanted to grow up to be like Kojima, and now I'm as far from him as a game writer can get. [90] [91]

---

90 **Ash:** You still pretty cool, though.

91 **Anthony:** Shut up, idiot.

THE END?

ASH

So, Anthony and I shit on *Metal Gear Solid* for about half of this book. If you're a fan of *MGS1*, you might be kind of pissed. But despite the amount of acid we spit at the game and its various baffling choices, despite the inordinately long cutscenes, the convoluted plot, and the awkward dialogue, we do love the game. It exploded our expectations of what a game could be. It challenged us both mechanically and intellectually. It took our little dense kiddie brains and pried them open just a touch wider.

It also holds such a dear place in my heart because of what it signifies in my own life: a friendship with my big brother. When I think of *Metal Gear Solid*, I think of summer afternoons with my brother, passing the controller back and forth, gasping at the same moments, laughing at the same clunky dialogue. And *MGS1* is *still* bringing us together, this time in the form of a creative project we can share. I owe a lot to this game.

That doesn't mean it's immune to my criticism. That doesn't mean it gets a free pass. That doesn't mean I can't point at it and say, "Stop it—you're being an idiot."

Because when you love something, you want it to be the best it can be. You want it to learn from its mistakes. You want it to grow and nurture others in the same way it nurtured you. When I picture the walls of Shadow Moses, when I see Snake's little polygonal form running through the snow, leaving footprints for baffled guards, I feel that warm bubbling of nostalgia in my chest. *Metal Gear Solid* means a lot to me. And that's why it's important that I call it on its nonsense.

Gamers are fiercely devoted people. We'll get in endless arguments about the endings of games, their mechanics, their price points, their voice actors, their plots, and their level design until our faces are blue, and then we'll keep talking. We collect art and action figures, we buy special editions, we get tattoos, we film fan vids. When we love, we love hard and we love deeply. And sometimes, when someone tells us that the thing we love is flawed, we get defensive. Because that's what happens when you love something—you want to defend it. You want to protect it.

If reading this book gave you a little bubble of hurt at the pit of your gut, I understand. Chances are, you love *MGS1* as much as Anthony and I do. You might even doubt that we care about it as much as we say we do. But we both believe that we have a responsibility to deconstruct the things we love, to try and point out how they could be more inclusive, more conscious, and just better.

Because the games of today are inspiring the game designers of tomorrow. And the game designers of tomorrow will make games for a new generation of players. And we should give them games that are even *better* than the games we got to play when we were young. We should create compelling, moving games that push creative boundaries. We should show girls that they can be heroes. We should show boys that they can be more than just machismo-fueled action-dudes.

We should want more.

But the only way we can do that is by pointing at something that isn't working, and naming it. We need to feel comfortable saying: I love this game, but it's sexist. I love this game, but it's racist. I love this game, but the story is atrocious. I love this game, but I don't see myself represented in it.

And when we hear a complaint like that about a game we love, we have to stop that little seed of defensiveness from spilling over into anger. We have to recognize that a critic's concern doesn't say anything about us, and it doesn't make us wrong for liking that game. We're all on the same team, and we're all just trying to make this medium the best it can be. For everyone.

So when I think about *Metal Gear Solid*, I think of David Hayter's gruff shouts, I think of eating pizza with my big brother, and I think of my realization of what I wanted to do with my life. I think of a flawed, dated, offensive, sexist, clunky, inspiring, engaging, nuanced, revolutionary, amazing game—one that will always be a huge part of my life.

NOTES?

Kojima's G4 interview was part of a 2004 episode of the show *Icons*, the episode itself called "Metal Gear Solid." It's archived here: http://bit.ly/1HVCL2Q.

Robert Yang's comments on immersive sims appeared on his Radiator Design Blog in a post entitled "Dark Past (part 2): On level design, hookers, cybernetic architecture, Tony Hawk and all that converges" (January 15, 2011) which can be found at http://bit.ly/1L9jRop.

Absolute PlayStation International reviewed *MGS1* in February 1999. Their review is archived at http://bit.ly/1fAApdn.

Tom Francis's 2011 PC Gamer review of *Deus Ex: Human Revolution* (94/100) is here: http://bit.ly/1IU0Eqv.

The 2013 vg247 interview with Kojima is called "'!' – The Hideo Kojima Interview" and it's available at http://bit.ly/1gvPT2B

The study Ashly did with Rosalind Wiseman is called "Curiosity, Courage & Camouflage: Revealing Gaming

Habits of Teen Girls," and was presented at the 2015 Game Developers Conference. You can watch the talk online: http://bit.ly/1O46XaW.

John Szczepaniak's 2012 interview with Jeremy Blaustein, "Jeremy Blaustein reflects on 25 years of the Snake," appeared in March 2012 at Harcore Gaming 101: http://bit.ly/1Rs6q8i.

ACKNOWLEDGEMENTS?

This book wouldn't have been possible without the following people:

Maxwell Neely-Cohen
Gabe Durham
Michael P. Williams
Erin Robinson
Matt Charles
Ryan Plummer
Joseph Michael Owens
Nick Sweeney
Jim Fingal
Adam Robinson
Ken Baumann

SPECIAL THANKS

For making our second season of books possible, Boss Fight Books would like to thank Ken Durham, Jakub Koziol, Cathy Durham, Maxwell Neely-Cohen, Adrian Purser, Kevin John Harty, Gustav Wedholm, Theodore Fox, Anders Ekermo, Jim Fasoline, Mohammed Taher, Joe Murray, Ethan Storeng, Bill Barksdale, Max Symmes, Philip J. Reed, Robert Bowling, Jason Morales, Keith Charles, and Asher Henderson.

ALSO FROM BOSS FIGHT BOOKS